Urania

Camille Flammarion

Alpha Editions

This edition published in 2024

ISBN : 9789362097286

Design and Setting By
Alpha Editions
www.alphaedis.com
Email - info@alphaedis.com

As per information held with us this book is in Public Domain.
This book is a reproduction of an important historical work. Alpha Editions uses the best technology to reproduce historical work in the same manner it was first published to preserve its original nature. Any marks or number seen are left intentionally to preserve its true form.

Contents

Part First. —◆— THE HEAVENLY MUSE. ....- 1 -
I. A DREAM OF YOUTH. ....- 3 -
II. UNKNOWN HUMANITIES. ....- 9 -
III. THE INFINITE VARIETY OF BEINGS. ....- 19 -
IV. ETERNITY AND THE INFINITE ....- 23 -
V. THE LIGHT OF THE PAST. ....- 30 -
Part Second. —◆— GEORGE SPERO.................................- 36 -
I. LIFE. ....- 38 -
II. THE APPARITION. ....- 46 -
III. "TO BE, OR NOT TO BE?" ....- 55 -
IV. AMOR. ....- 66 -
V. THE AURORA BOREALIS. ....- 77 -
VI. ETERNAL PROGRESS. ....- 84 -
Part Third. —◆— HEAVEN AND EARTH.........................- 87 -
I. TELEPATHY. ....- 88 -
II. ITER EXTATICUM CŒLESTE. ....- 113 -
III. THE PLANET MARS. ....- 125 -
IV. THE FIXED POINT IN THE UNIVERSE. ....- 140 -
A SOUL CLOTHED WITH AIR. ....- 150 -
V. AD VERITATEM PER SCIENTIAM............................- 161 -
Footnotes...- 168 -

Part First.
THE HEAVENLY MUSE.

I.
A DREAM OF YOUTH.

I WAS seventeen years old; her name was Urania.

Was Urania a fair, blue-eyed maiden, a dream of spring, an innocent but inquisitive daughter of Eve? No; she was simply, as in days of yore, that one of the nine Muses who presided over astronomy, and whose celestial glance inspired and directed the chorus of the spheres; she was the angelic idea which soars above terrestrial dulness. She had not the disturbing flesh, nor the heart whose palpitations are communicated at a distance, nor the gentle ardor of human life; but she existed nevertheless in a sort of ideal world,—lofty and always pure,—and yet she was human enough in name and form to produce a strong and deep impression upon an adolescent soul, to arouse in that soul an indefinite, indefinable feeling of admiration,—almost of love.

In his hours of solitude, and even through the intellectual labors with which the education of the day overloads his brain, a young man whose hand has never plucked the divine fruit from the tree of Paradise, whose lips are still untouched, whose heart has not yet spoken, whose senses are beginning to awaken amid vague new aspirations, thrills with a presentiment of the divinity to which he is soon to sacrifice, and personifies beforehand in ever-varying forms the unknown being who floats through the airy fabric of his dreams. He wishes, longs to reach this unknown being, but dares not yet, perhaps may never dare, in the purity of his admiration, unless some helping hand come to his aid. If Chloe is not well informed, indiscreet and talkative Lycinion must take it upon herself to instruct Daphnis.

Whatever tells us of the yet unknown attraction can charm, interest, delight, and captivate us. A cold engraving, showing the oval of a pure face, even an old-fashioned painting, a sculpture,—a sculpture especially,—awakens a new feeling in our hearts; the blood flows faster, or seems to stop; the idea crosses our reddening brow like a flash, and remains floating in our pensive mind. It is the beginning of desires, the beginning of life, the dawn of a beautiful summer day, harbinger of the sunrise.

As for me, my first love, my adolescent passion, had, not for its object assuredly, but as a determining cause—a clock! It is rather odd, but so it is! Humdrum calculations used up all my afternoons from two until four; it was merely correcting observations, made the night before, of stars or planets by applying the reductions arising from atmospheric refraction, which itself depends on the height of the barometer and the temperature. These calculations are as simple as they are tiresome; they are made mechanically, by the help of prepared tables, while thinking of something else.

The illustrious Le Verrier was then director of the Paris Observatory. Although in no way artistic, he had in his study a golden bronze clock of very beautiful design, dating from the end of the First Empire,—the work of Pradier's chisel. The pedestal of this clock represented in bas-relief the birth of astronomy on the Egyptian plains. A massive celestial sphere surrounded by the zodiacal circle, supported by sphinxes, held the dial; Egyptian gods adorned the sides. But the chief beauty of this artistic work consisted of an exquisite little statue of Urania, lithe, elegant,—I had almost said majestic.

The celestial Muse was standing. With her right hand she measured the degrees of the starry sphere by the aid of a compass; her drooping left hand held a small astronomical telescope. Superbly draped, she looked down in an attitude of stately grandeur. I had never before seen so beautiful a face as hers. With the light falling directly upon it, the pure countenance looked grave and austere. If the light came to it obliquely, it appeared somewhat meditative; but coming from above and from the side, the enchanting face brightened with a mysterious smile, her glance grew almost caressing, her exquisite serenity gave place to an expression of joy, amiability, and happiness delightful to contemplate. It was like a song of the soul, a poetic melody. These changes of expression fairly made the statue alive. Muse and goddess, she was beautiful, she was enchanting, she was adorable.

Whenever I had occasion to go to the eminent mathematician it was not his world-wide reputation which impressed me most. I forgot the formulas of logarithms, and even the immortal discovery of the planet Neptune, to bow beneath the charm of Pradier's work. The beautiful figure so admirably modelled beneath its antique drapery, the graceful throat, the expressive face, attracted my eyes and captivated my thoughts. Very often, as we were leaving the office about four o'clock to go back to Paris, I would peep through the half-open door to see if the director were absent. Monday and Wednesday were the best days,—the first because of the Institute meetings, which he seldom missed; the second on account of the Bureau of Longitudes sessions, which he avoided with the most profound disdain: he would even leave the observatory expressly, to make his contempt for them more emphatic. Then I would stand before my dear Urania and look at her to my heart's content, enraptured by her beauty of form and face, and go away more satisfied, but not happier,—she charmed, but filled me with regrets.

One evening—the evening on which I discovered how the light could change her face—I found the library-door wide open. A lamp stood on the chimney-piece shedding its rays over the Muse in one of her most bewitching aspects. The slanting light lovingly caressed the brow, cheeks, lips, and throat. Her expression was wonderful. I went in, and for a while stood there in motionless contemplation. Then I tried changing the position of the lamp, making the light play over the shoulders, arms, neck, and hair. The statue seemed to live, to think, to awake, and smile again! Odd, whimsical idea; strange feeling! I had actually fallen in love! I had changed from admirer to lover! If I had been told then that what I felt was not real love, and that this platonism was but a childish dream, I should have been very incredulous. The director came in, but did not seem so much surprised at my presence as I might have feared. (The study was often used to reach the observation rooms.) "You are late for Jupiter," he said, as I replaced the lamp on the chimney-piece; and when I reached the threshold he added, "Can it be possible that you are a poet?" lengthening out the last syllable as though he had said "poët."

I might have answered him by quoting Kepler, Galileo, D'Alembert, the two Herschels, and other famous savants who were poets and astronomers at the same time. I could have reminded him that the first director of this very observatory, Jean-Dominique Cassini, sang of Urania in Latin, French, and Italian verse. But the observatory pupils were not in the habit of answering the senator-director in any way whatever; senators were personages of importance in those days, and the directorship of the observatory was a life-office. Then too the great geometrician would have looked upon the most wonderful poem by Dante, Ariosto, or Hugo with the same profound disdain that a big Newfoundland dog would show if one should put a glass of wine to his mouth. Besides, I was clearly in the wrong.

How that charming figure of Urania haunted me, with all the delicious changes of expression! Her smile was so gracious, and sometimes her bronze eyes had such a real look. She lacked nothing but speech.

That night, just as I fell asleep, I saw the divine goddess again; and this time she spoke.

Oh, she was really living now! And what a pretty mouth! I could have kissed each word. "Come," she said, "come up into the sky. Far away from the earth, you shall look down upon this lower world, you shall contemplate the great universe in its grandeur. Come and see."

II.
UNKNOWN HUMANITIES.

THEN I saw the Earth sinking down into the yawning depths of immensity; the cupolas of the observatory, Paris with its lights, were rapidly fading away. Although feeling as if I were motionless, I had the same sensation which one experiences on rising in a balloon and seeing the earth descend. I went up, up, in a magic flight toward the inaccessible zenith. Urania was with me, a little higher up, looking at me kindly and pointing out the kingdoms below. Day had come again. I recognized France, the Rhine, Germany, Austria, Italy, the Mediterranean, Spain, the Atlantic Ocean, the Channel, England. But all this liliputian geography soon shrank away. Speedily the terrestrial globe was reduced to the dimensions of the moon in its last quarter; then to a little full moon.

"There," said she, "is the famous terrestrial globe on which so many passions stir, within whose narrow limits the thought of so many millions of human beings is confined, whose sight cannot extend beyond it. See how its apparent size diminishes as our horizon develops. We can no longer distinguish Europe from Asia; and there is North America. How very small it all is!"

As we passed through the Moon's neighborhood I had noticed our satellite's hilly landscapes, the mountain crests radiant with light, deep valleys filled with shadows, and I should have liked to stop for a nearer study of the surroundings; but Urania did not deign to bestow so much as a passing glance at it, and drew me on in a rapid flight toward the sidereal regions.

We were still ascending. The Earth grew smaller and smaller as we receded from it, until it looked like a simple star shining from solar illumination on the bosom of dark and empty space. We turned toward the Sun, which shone in space, but without filling it with light, so that we could see stars and planets at the same time, no longer obscured by its rays, because it could not illumine empty space. The angelic goddess showed me Mercury, in close neighborhood to the Sun, Venus, shining on the other side, the Earth, equalling Venus in appearance and brilliancy, Mars, whose inland seas and canals I recognized, Jupiter, with its four enormous moons, Saturn, Uranus. "All these worlds," said she, "are upheld in vacancy by the attraction of the Sun, around which they revolve with great speed. It is an harmonious choir gravitating about its centre. The Earth is but a floating island, a little hamlet of this great solar country; and the solar empire itself is but a little province on the breast of sidereal vastness."

We rose still higher. The Sun and its system were rapidly passing. The Earth was but a little spot now; Jupiter himself, that colossal world, had melted away, like Mars and Venus, to a tiny little dot scarcely larger than the Earth. We passed within sight of Saturn, surrounded by his gigantic rings, whose study alone would be sufficient to prove the immense and unimaginable variety reigning in the universe. Saturn is a whole system in itself, with its rings composed of particles torn from it in its dizzy revolution, and with its eight satellites accompanying it like a celestial retinue.

As we soared aloft, our Sun decreased in grandeur. Soon it had descended to the rank of a planet, then lost all majesty, all superiority over the sidereal population, and was nothing more than a star, scarcely more brilliant than the others. I looked about me at all this vast extent, on whose spangled bosom we were still going upward, and tried to recognize the constellations; but their forms were beginning to change perceptibly, from the lengthening perspective caused by my journey. I thought I could see that our Sun had insensibly dwindled to a tiny star and joined the constellation of the Centaur; while a new light, pale, bluish, and very strange, seemed to greet me from the direction toward which Urania was bearing me. This new brightness had nothing terrestrial about it, and reminded me of no effect that I had ever seen on the Earth among the changing tints of the sunset after a storm, or in the undefined mists of morning, or during the calm and silent moonlight hours on the mirror of the sea. This last effect is nearer its appearance; but the strange light was, and became more and more, of a real blue,—blue, not like a reflection of celestial azure, nor like a contrast analogous to that produced by an electric light compared with gas, but blue, as if the Sun itself were blue.

Imagine my amazement when I discovered that we were approaching the influence of an absolutely blue sun, like a shining disk, which might have been cut from one of our most beautiful terrestrial skies, standing out luminously upon a perfectly black background all thickly studded with stars. This sapphire sun was the centre of a planetary system lighted by its rays. We were to pass quite near one of the planets. The blue sun increased perceptibly in size; but—another phenomenon as singular as the first—the light it threw upon this planet seemed to be tinged on one side with green. I looked into the sky again, and saw a second sun,—this one a beautiful emerald green. I could not believe my eyes!

Urania said: "We are crossing the solar system of Gamma Andromedæ, of which you see but one part as yet; for it is made up, not of these two suns, but in reality of three,—one blue, one green, and one orange yellow. The blue sun, which is the smallest, turns around the green sun; and the latter gravitates with its companion around the great orange sun, which you will perceive in an instant."

Sure enough! A second later I saw a third sun, colored with a glowing radiancy, whose contrast with its two companions produced a most dazzling illumination. I knew about this interesting sidereal system from having observed it more than once through the telescope; but I had never suspected its real splendor. What fiery depths! what scintillations! what brilliancy of color in that strange source of blue light in the second sun's green illumination and the tawny, golden effulgence of the third!

But, as I have said, we were approaching one of the worlds belonging to the system of the sapphire sun. Everything was blue,—landscapes, water, plants, rocks,—slightly greenish on the side lighted by the second sun, and hardly touched by the rays of the orange sun, which was rising on the distant horizon. As we floated into the atmosphere of this world a soft, delicious music was wafted into the air like a perfume, a dream. Never had I heard anything like it. The sweet, deep, distant melody seemed to come from a choir of harps and violins, strengthened by an accompaniment of organs. It was an exquisite anthem, which charmed at once; it needed no analyzing to be understood; it filled the soul with ecstasy. It seemed to me that I could have lingered there listening for an eternity. I was so fearful of losing a single note that I dared not speak to my guide. Urania noticed it; stretching out her hand toward a lake, she pointed to a group of winged beings who were hovering over the blue waters.

They had not the earthly human form. They were beings who had evidently been created to live in air. They seemed woven out of light. At a distance I thought they were dragon-flies; they had their slender, graceful shape, the same wide wings, quickness, and lightness. But on examining them more closely I noticed their height, which was not inferior to our own, and realized from the expression of their eyes that they were not animals. Their heads were very like that of the dragon-fly, and like those aerial creatures they had no legs. The delicious music to which I had been listening was but the noise of their flight. They were very numerous,—perhaps many thousands.

From the mountain-tops could be seen plants which were neither trees nor flowers, whose slender stalks rose to an enormous height; the branched stems bearing, as though with outstretched arms, great tulip-shaped cups. These plants were alive, or as much so as our sensitive growths, perhaps more, and like the *desmodium*, with its moving leaves, showed their internal impressions by their motions. These groves formed actual vegetable cities. The inhabitants of this world had no other dwellings, but reposed among the fragrant sensitive-plants when not floating in the air.

"This seems a very strange world to you," said Urania; "you are wondering what kinds of ideas, habits, or history these people could have,—what kinds of arts, literature, and sciences. It would take a long time to answer all the questions you might ask. Know only that their eyes are superior to your finest telescopes; that their nervous system vibrates at the passing of a comet, and discovers by an electric sense facts which you on the Earth will never know. The organs which you see under their wings serve as hands, more skilful than yours. Instead of printing, they take the direct photography of events and the phonetic impression of words. They care very little for anything but scientific research; that is to say, the study of Nature. The three passions which absorb the greater part of earthly life—eager greed for fortune, political ambition, and love—are unknown to them, because they require nothing to live on, there are no international divisions nor government, except a council of administration, and because they are androgynous."

"Androgynous!" I repeated; and ventured to add, "Is that best?"

"It is *different*. It is a great deal of trouble saved to a humanity."

"To be in a condition to understand the infinite diversity displayed in the different phases of creation," she continued, "it is necessary to cast aside all terrestrial feelings and ideas. Just as the species of your planet have changed in succeeding ages from the uncouth creatures of the first geological periods to the appearance of man, and as even now the animal and vegetable population of the Earth is still composed of the most widely varying forms, from man to the coral, from bird to fish, from an elephant to a butterfly, so on an incomparably vaster scale the forces of Nature have given birth to an infinite diversity of beings and things throughout the innumerable worlds of heaven. The form of its occupant is the result in each world of some element peculiar to that globe,—substance, heat, light, electricity, density, weight. Shape, functions, the number of the senses,—you have but five, and they are rather poor ones,—depend on the vital conditions of each sphere. Life is earthly on the Earth, Martial on Mars, Saturnian on Saturn, Neptunian on Neptune,—that is to say, appropriate to each habitation; or, to express it better, more strictly speaking, produced and developed by each world according to its organic condition, and following a primordial law which all Nature obeys,—the law of progress."

While she was speaking I had watched the flight of the aerial creatures toward the city of flowers, and saw with astonishment that the plants were moving, raising or lowering themselves to receive them. The green sun had sunk beneath the horizon, and the yellow sun had risen in the sky; the landscape was suffused with a fairy-like tinge, over which hung an enormous half-green, half-orange moon. Then the infinite melody which had been filling the air died away, and amid a profound silence I heard a song arise from so pure a voice that no human tones could be compared with it.

"What a marvellous system!" I cried,—"a world illumined by such glowing lights! It is having a close view of double, triple, and multiple stars."

"Splendid suns those stars," she answered, "gracefully united in the bonds of a mutual attraction; from the Earth you see them cradled two and two on the bosom of the sky, always beautiful, pure, and luminous. Hanging in the infinite, they lean to each other, but never touch, as though their union, more moral than material, were ordered by an invisible and superior power, and following harmonious curves, they gravitate in cadence around each other,—

celestial couples which blossomed at the spring-time of creation in the constellated meadows of infinity. While simple suns like yours shine in the deserts of space solitary, fixed, and undisturbed, double and multiple suns seem to enliven the silent regions of the eternal void by their motion, color, and life. These sidereal time-keepers mark the centuries and eras of other worlds for you.

"But," she added, "let us continue our journey; we are but a few trillion leagues from the Earth."

"A few *trillion*?"

"Yes. If we could hear the sounds of your planet from here,—its volcanoes, cannonadings, and thunders, or the wild vociferations of its crowds in times of revolution, or the hymns which rise to heaven from the churches,—the distance is so great that, even admitting that the noises could surmount it with the speed of sound in the air, it would require not less than fifteen million years to reach here. We could hear to-day only what took place on Earth fifteen million years ago. And yet, compared with the immensity of the universe, we are still very near your home.

"You can still distinguish your Sun yonder,—that tiny little star. We have not been out of the universe to which it, with its system of planets, belongs. That universe is composed of several thousand milliards of suns, separated from each other by trillions of leagues. Its extent is so vast that it would take a flash of lightning fifteen thousand years to cross it, travelling at the rate of three hundred thousand kilometres a second.

"And suns everywhere, on all sides! In whatever direction we look, all about us are sources of light, heat, and life in inexhaustible variety,—suns of every lustre, of all magnitudes, all ages, upheld in the eternal void, in the luminous ether, by the mutual attraction of all and the motion of each. Your Sun moves and bears you away toward the constellation of Hercules; that one, whose system we have just crossed, goes south toward the Pleiades; Sirius hurries away toward the Dove; Pollux whirls swiftly toward the Milky Way. All these millions, these thousands of millions, of suns hasten through boundless space with a speed which attains a velocity of two, three, and even four thousand metres a second. Motion maintains the equilibrium of the universe, and constitutes its organization, energy, and life."

III.
THE INFINITE VARIETY OF BEINGS.

THE tricolored system had long since disappeared in our upward flight. We were passing through the neighborhood of a great many worlds which were very different from our Earth. Some of them appeared to be entirely covered with water, and peopled by aquatic beings; others, occupied entirely by plants. We stopped near several of them. What unimaginable variety! The inhabitants of one of them seemed to me especially beautiful. Urania apprised me of the fact that their organization was totally different from that of the children of Earth, and that those human beings could discern the physico-chemical operations which take place in the maintenance of the body. In our earthly organism we do not see, for example, how the food absorbed is assimilated,—how the blood, tissues, and bones renew themselves; all functions are fulfilled instinctively, without thought perceiving it. Thus man suffers from a thousand maladies whose origin is hidden, and often undiscoverable. There the human being feels the action of his vital nourishment as we feel pleasure or pain. A nerve starts from every particle of his body, so to speak, which transmits the different impressions it receives to the brain. If terrestrial man were endowed with such a nervous system, looking into his organism through the intermediary of the nerves, he would see how food transforms itself into chyle, the latter into blood, blood into flesh, muscular, nervous substance, etc.: he would see himself! But we are very far from that, the centre of our perceptions being obstructed by nerves, thickened by cerebral lobes and optic thalami.

On another globe which we crossed during the night—that is to say, on the side of its nocturnal hemisphere—human eyes are so constructed as to be *luminous*, and shine as though some phosphorescent emanation radiated from their strange centres. A night meeting comprising a large number of these persons presents an extremely fantastic appearance, because the brilliancy, as well as the color, of the eyes changes with the different passions by which they are swayed. More than that, the power of their glance is such that they exert an *electric* and magnetic influence of variable intensity, and which under certain conditions has the effect of lightning, causing the victim upon whom the force and energy of their will is fixed to fall dead.

A little farther away my celestial guide pointed out a world in which organisms enjoy a precious faculty: the soul may change its body without passing through the often disagreeable and always sad experience of death. A savant who has labored all his life for the instruction of mankind, and feels that his end is drawing near before he has been able to complete his noble undertaking, can change bodies with a youth, and begin a new life still more useful than the first. The young man's consent and the magnetic manipulation of a competent physician are sufficient for the transmigration. Sometimes it happens that two persons united by the sweet, strong ties of love effect such an exchange of bodies after a union of many years,—the husband's soul takes the wife's body, and conversely, for the rest of their existence. The inmost experience of life becomes incomparably more complete for each of them. Savants and historians desirous of living two centuries instead of one, are seen to fall into a long artificial winter's sleep, which suspends their lives for half of each year, and even more. Some even succeed in living three times longer than the normal life of centenarians.

A few seconds later, crossing another system, we met a kind of organism still more different from ours, and assuredly far superior. With the inhabitants of the planet we were then looking at,—a world lighted by a brilliant hydrogenized sun,—thought is not obliged to pass through speech to be understood. How many times has it not happened when a bright or transcendent idea came into our minds, and we wanted to utter it or write it out, that just as we were about to speak or write, we felt that it was slipping away, flying from us, confused or metamorphosed into something else? The inhabitants of this planet have a sixth sense, which might be called magneto-telegraphic, by virtue of which, when the author is not disinclined, the thought becomes outwardly manifest, and can be read upon a feature which occupies very much the same place as a forehead. These silent conversations are often the deepest and most enjoyable,—always the most sincere.

We are innocently disposed to believe that the human organism is perfect, and leaves nothing on earth to be desired; but for all that have we not often regretted being obliged to listen, in spite of ourselves, to disagreeable words, absurd speeches, a sermon verbose with emptiness, bad music, slander, or calumny? Our grammars vainly pretend that we can "close our ears" to these speeches; unfortunately there is no such thing. You cannot shut your ears as you can your eyes. I was very much surprised to find a planet where Nature had not forgotten this salutary provision. As we stopped there for an instant, Urania pointed out ears which closed like eyelids. "There is very much less anger and vexation here than with you," said she; "but the wranglings of political parties are much more sharp and vociferous, adversaries are unwilling to listen to disputes, and succeed effectually, notwithstanding the speakers may be most loquacious."

On another world, in which phosphorus plays a large part, whose atmosphere is constantly electrified, whose temperature is very high, and where the inhabitants have no sufficient reason for inventing wearing apparel, certain passions manifest themselves by the illumination of some part of the body. It is the same thing on a large scale that we see in our terrestrial meadows on a smaller one in mild summer evenings when glow-worms silently manifest themselves, and then waste away in a soft, amorous flame. It is very curious to observe the appearance of these luminous couples in the evening in populous cities. The color of the phosphorescence differs in the sexes, and its intensity varies with the age and temperament. The stronger sex burns with a more or less ardent red flame, and the gentler sex with a bluish light, sometimes pale and diaphanous. Our glow-worms, however, give but a very faint and rudimentary idea respecting the nature of the impressions experienced by these peculiar beings. I could not believe my eyes when we were passing through the atmosphere of this planet. But I was still more surprised on arriving at the satellite of this unique world. That was a solitary moon, lighted by a kind of twilight sun. A sombre valley lay before us. From the trees scattered on both slopes of the valley hung human beings enveloped in shrouds. They had tied themselves to the branches by their hair, and were sleeping in the deepest silence. What I had taken for grave-clothes was a covering formed from the growth of their bleached and tangled locks. As I was wondering at this marvellous spectacle Urania told me this was their usual mode of interment and resurrection. Yes, on this world human beings enjoyed the organic faculty of those insects which have the gift of going to sleep in a chrysalis state, and metamorphosing themselves into winged butterflies. It is like a double human race; and the beings in the first phase, even the coarsest and most material of them, need but to die to rise again in the most splendid of transformations. Each year in this world represents about two hundred terrestrial years. Two thirds of the year is lived in the lower condition, one third (winter) in the chrysalis state, and the following spring the sleepers feel life coming back to their transformed flesh; they stir, awaken, leave their fleecy coverings on the trees, and freeing themselves from them, fly away, wonderful winged creatures, to aerial regions, there to live for a new Phœnician year,—that is, for two hundred years of our swiftly moving planet.

We crossed a great number of planets in this way, and it seemed as though all eternity would not be long enough to admit of my enjoying these creations unknown to earth; but my guide barely left me time to realize this, and still new suns and new worlds were appearing. We were very near striking against some transparent comets in our rapid flight, that were wandering about like a breath from one system to another, and more than once I felt myself strongly attracted toward wonderful planets with fresh landscapes, whose occupants would have been new objects of study. And yet the celestial Muse bore me on without fatigue still higher, still farther away, until at last we came to what seemed to me the confines of the universe. The suns grew more rare, less luminous, paler; darkness was more intense between the stars; and we were soon in the midst of an actual desert, the thousands of millions of stars which constitute the universe visible from the Earth being far distant: everything had faded to a little, lonely Milky Way in empty infinity.

"At last we have reached the very limits of creation!" I cried.

"Look!" she replied, pointing to the zenith.

IV.
ETERNITY AND THE INFINITE

WHAT was that? Could it be true? Another universe was coming down to us! Millions and millions of suns grouped together were floating about like a celestial archipelago, and as we flew toward them they spread themselves out like a limitless cloud of stars. I looked about me on all sides, trying to pierce the depths of boundless space, and saw similar clusters of twinkling stars scattered about in all directions, at various distances.

The new universe which we were entering was made up principally of red, ruby, and garnet suns. Many of them were absolutely blood-red.

It was like going through a magnificent display of lightning. We sped swiftly from sun to sun; but incessant electrical commotions like the flashes of an aurora-borealis assailed us on all sides. What strange abiding-places worlds lighted solely by red suns must be! Then, too, we saw in one section of this universe a secondary group, composed of great numbers of rose-colored and blue stars. Suddenly an enormous comet, whose head was like some monster's open jaws, rushed upon and enveloped us. I clung terror-stricken to my goddess's side, who was for a moment hidden from me by a luminous haze. We were soon in a dark desert again, for the second universe, like the first, was now far away.

*****

"Creation," she said, "comprises an infinite number of distinct worlds, separated from each other by abysses of vacancy."

"An *infinite* number?"

"A mathematical objection," she answered. "Doubtless, no matter how great a number may be, it cannot be actually infinite, since by thought one can always increase by a unit, or even double, treble, centuple it. But remember that the present is but a door through which the future rushes to the past. Eternity is endless, and the number of the worlds will be like it, without end."

"Look! You still see, always and on all sides, new celestial archipelagoes,— new worlds everywhere."

"It seems to me, O Urania! that we have been ascending toward the boundless heavens for a long time, and at very great speed."

"We could rise like this forever," she answered, "and never reach a definite limit.

"We could be wafted about yonder to right, to left; forward, backward; above, below,—in no matter what direction, but never anywhere should we find any confines.

"Never, never any end!

"Do you know where we are? Do you know how we reached here?

"We are—on the threshold of the infinite, as we were when on the Earth. *We have not advanced one step!*"

*****

A deep emotion had taken possession of my mind. Urania's last words had pierced my very marrow like an icy chill. "Never any end—never! never," I repeated; I could think or speak of nothing else. But still the magnificence of the spectacle appealed to my eyes, and my feeling of annihilation gave place to enthusiasm.

"Astronomy," I cried, "is everything! To know these things, to live in the infinite,—oh, Urania! what are other human ideas compared with science? Shadows, phantoms!"

"Oh! you will wake up again upon the Earth," she said; "you will admire, and rightly too, the wisdom of your masters. But understand this,—the astronomy of your schools and observatories, mathematical astronomy, the beautiful science as known to Newton, Laplace, Le Verrier, is not yet definite, actual knowledge.

"That, O my son! is not the end which I have pursued since the days of Hipparchus and Ptolemy. Look at the thousands of suns analogous to that which gives life to the earth, which like it are sources of light, motion, activity, and splendor! Ah! that is the object of the science to come,—the study of universal and eternal life. Until now, no one has ever entered the temple. Figures are not an end, but a means; they do not represent Nature's structure, only the methods, the scaffoldings. You are to see the dawn of a new day. Mathematical astronomy will yield her place to physical astronomy, to the true study of Nature.

"Yes," she continued, "astronomers who calculate the movements of the stars in their daily passage of the meridian, those who foretell eclipses, celestial phenomena, periodical comets, who observe the exact positions of the stars and planets on the different degrees of the celestial sphere so carefully; those who discover comets, planets, satellites, and variable stars; those who investigate and determine the disturbance caused the Earth's motion by attraction from the Moon and planets; those who consecrate their night-watches to the discovery of the fundamental elements of the world's system,—are all of them calculators and observers, precursors of the new astronomy. These are immense labors, studies worthy of admiration, and important works which bring to light the highest faculties of the human mind. But it is the army of the past; mathematicians and geometricians. Henceforth, the hearts of savants will throb for a still nobler conquest. All these great minds never really left the Earth while studying the skies. Astronomy's aim is not to show us the apparent position of shining specks, nor to weigh stones moving through space, nor to foretell eclipses, or the phases of the Moon or tides. All this is fine, but it is not enough.

"If life did not exist upon the earth, that planet would be absolutely devoid of interest for any mind whatsoever; and the same remark is applicable to all the worlds which gravitate around the thousands of millions of suns in the wide stretches of immensity. Life is the object of the whole creation. If there were neither life nor thought, it would all be null and void.

"You are destined to witness an entire transformation in science. Matter will give place to mind."

"Life universal!" I asked: "Are all the planets of our solar system inhabited? Are the myriads of worlds which people the infinite lived upon? Do those forms of human life resemble ours? Shall we ever know them?"

"The epoch of your life upon the earth, even the duration of terrestrial humanity, is but a moment in eternity."

I did not understand this answer to my questions.

"There is no reason why all the worlds should be inhabited *now*," she went on. "The present period is of no more importance than those which preceded or will follow it.

"The length of the Earth's existence will be longer—much longer, perhaps ten times longer—than that of its vital human period. Out of a dozen worlds selected by chance from immensity, we could, for example, find hardly one inhabited by a really intelligent race. Some have been already, others will be in the future; these are in preparation, those have run through all their phases: here cradles, there graves. And then too an infinite variety in the forces of Nature and their manifestations is revealed; earthly life being in no way the type of extra-terrestrial existence. Beings can think, live, in wholly different organizations from those with which you are familiar on your own planet. Inhabitants of the other worlds have neither your form nor senses; they are otherwise.

"The day will come, and very soon, since you are called to see it, when the study of the conditions of life in the various provinces of the universe will be astronomy's essential aim and chief charm. Soon, instead of being concerned simply about the distance, the motion, and the material facts of your neighboring planets, astronomers will discover their physical constitution,—for example, their geographical appearance, their climatology, their meteorology,—will solve the mystery of their vital organizations, and will discuss their inhabitants. They will find that Mars and Venus are actually peopled by thinking beings; that Jupiter is still in its primary period of organic preparation; that Saturn looks down upon us under quite different conditions from those which were instrumental in the establishment of terrestrial life, and without passing through a state analogous to that of Earth, will be inhabited by beings incompatible with earthly organisms. New methods will tell about the physical and chemical constitutions of the stars and the nature of their atmospheres. Perfected instruments will permit the discovery of direct proofs of existence in these planetary humanities and the idea of putting one's self in communication with them. This is the scientific transformation which will mark the close of the nineteenth century and inaugurate the twentieth."

I listened with delight to these words of the celestial Muse, which shed an entirely different light upon the future of astronomy and filled me with renewed ardor. Before my eyes was a panorama of innumerable worlds moving in space, and I understood that the true object of science is to teach us about those far distant universes and allow us to live in those wide horizons. The beautiful goddess resumed:

"Astronomy's mission will be still higher. After making you know and feel that the Earth is but a city in the celestial country, and man a citizen of heaven, she will go still farther. Disclosing the plan on which the physical universe is constructed, she will show that the moral universe is constructed on the very same basis, that the two worlds form but one world, and that mind governs matter. What she will have done for space she will do for time. After realizing the boundlessness of space, and recognizing that the same laws govern all places simultaneously and make the vast universe one grand unit, you will learn that the centuries of the past and of the future are linked with the present, and that thinking monads will live forever through successive and progressive changes. You will learn that minds exist incomparably superior to the greatest minds of earthly humanity, and that all things advance toward supreme perfection. You will learn too that the material form is but an appearance, and that the real being consists of an imponderable, intangible, and invisible form.

"Astronomy will then be eminently and above all else the directress of philosophy. Those who reason without astronomical knowledge will never reach the truth. Those who follow her beacon faithfully will gradually rise to the solutions of the greatest problems.

"Astronomical philosophy will be the religion of lofty minds.

"You will see this double transformation in science," she added, "when you leave the terrestrial globe; the astronomical knowledge which you already so justly prize will be entirely remodelled in form as well as spirit.

"But this is not all. The renewal of an old science will be of little use to mankind in general if these sublime truths which develop the mind, enlighten the soul, and free it from vulgar common-place should be kept shut up within the narrow limits of professional astronomers. This time too will pass away. We must begin anew. The torch must be taken in hand, and its glory increased by carrying it into the busy streets and public squares. Every one is called to receive the light, every one is thirsting for it,—especially the humble, those on whom fortune frowns, for these are the persons who think most; these are eager for knowledge, while the contented ones of the century do not suspect their own ignorance, and are almost proud of staying in it. Yes, the light of astronomy must be diffused throughout the world; it must filter through the strata of humanity to the popular masses, enlighten their consciences, elevate their hearts. That will be its most beautiful and its grandest, greatest mission!"

V.
THE LIGHT OF THE PAST.

THUS spoke my celestial guide. Her face was glorious as the day, her eyes shone with a starry lustre, her voice was like divine music. I looked at the worlds about us revolving in space, and felt that a mighty harmony controlled the course of Nature.

"Now let us return to the Earth," she said, pointing to the spot where our terrestrial Sun had disappeared. "But look again. You understand now that space is infinite; you will soon comprehend that time is eternal."

We crossed other constellations and came back toward the solar system. I saw the Sun reappear, looking like a little star.

"For an instant," said she, "I am going to give you, if not divine, at least angelic sight. Your soul shall feel the ethereal vibrations which constitute light itself, and shall know that the history of each world is eternal with God. To see is to know: behold!"

Just as a microscope shows us an ant as large as an elephant, and penetrates the infinitely small, making the invisible visible, so at the Muse's command my sight suddenly acquired an unknown power of perception, and distinguished the Earth in space, very near the Sun, which was in eclipse, and from invisible it became visible.

I recognized it; and as I watched, its disk grew larger, looking like the Moon a few days before the full. After a while I could distinguish the principal geographical aspects in the growing disk,—the snowy patch at the North Pole, the outlines of Europe and Asia, the North Sea, the Atlantic, the Mediterranean. The more steadily I fixed my gaze, the better I could see. Details became more and more perceptible, as if I were gradually changing the lenses of a microscope. I recognized the geographical form of France; but our beautiful country appeared to be entirely green,—from the Rhine to the Ocean, from the Channel to the Mediterranean, as if it were covered with one immense forest. I succeeded, however, better and better in distinguishing the slightest details, for the Alps, the Pyrenees, the Rhine, the Rhone, the Loire, were easily found.

"Pay great attention," murmured my companion.

As she said this, she placed the tips of her slender fingers lightly on my brow, as though she had wished to magnetize my brain and endow my perceptive faculties with still greater power. Then I looked again more intently at the vision, and saw before my eyes Gaul in the time of Julius Cæsar. It was during the war of independence aroused by the patriotism of Vercingetorix.

"We are at such a distance from the Earth," said Urania, "that light requires all the time that separates us from Julius Cæsar to reach here. Only the rays of light that left the Earth at that time come to us; and yet light travels at the rate of three hundred thousand kilometres a second. It is fast, very fast, but it is not instantaneous. Astronomers on the Earth, who are observing stars situated as far from them as we are now, do not see them as they really are, but as they were when the rays of light which they see to-day left them; that is to say, as they were more than eighteen centuries ago.

"One never sees the stars from the Earth, nor from any point in space, as they are, but as they have been," she continued; "the farther away from them one is, the more behind he is in their history.

"You observe most carefully through the telescope stars which no longer exist. Many of the stars visible to the naked eye are no longer in existence. Many of the nebulæ whose substance you analyze through the spectroscope have become suns. Many of your most beautiful red stars are extinct and dead; you would not detect them if you should go to them.

"The light shed from all the suns which people immensity, the light reflected into space from all the worlds irradiated by these suns, carries away through the boundless skies photographs of all the centuries every day, every second. Looking at a star, you see it as it was at the time the impression that you receive left it,—just as when you hear a clock strike, you receive the sound after it has left it, and as long after as you are far from it.

"The result is, that the history of all these worlds actually travels through space, never entirely disappearing; that all past events are present and indestructible in the bosom of the infinite.

"The universe will endure forever. The Earth will come to an end, and some day will be nothing but a tomb. But there will be new suns and new earths, new springs and new smiles, and life will always bloom afresh in the limitless and endless universe.

"I wanted to show you," said she, after a pause, "how eternal time is! You have felt the infinity of space, you have understood the grandeur of the universe. Now your celestial journey is over. We must go back to the earth and your own home again.

"For yourself," she added, "know that study is the one source of any intellectual value; be neither rich nor poor; keep yourself from all ambition as well as from all servitude; be independent,—independence is the rarest gift and the first condition of happiness."

Urania was still speaking in her gentle voice; but my brain was so confused by the commotion aroused in it by so many extraordinary scenes that I was seized by a fit of trembling. A shiver ran over me from head to foot, which was probably the cause of my abrupt awakening in a state of great agitation. Alas! the delightful celestial journey had ended.

I looked about for Urania, but could not find her. A bright moonbeam shining through my bedroom window lightly touched the edge of a curtain and seemed vaguely to outline the aerial form of my heavenly guide; but it was only a moonbeam.

*****

When I went back to the observatory the next morning, my first impulse was to find some pretext for going to the director's study to see the charming Muse again who had rewarded me by such a dream....

The clock had disappeared!

In its place stood a white marble bust of the illustrious astronomer.

I looked through the other rooms, even the private apartments, under a thousand different excuses; but she was nowhere to be found.

I searched for days and weeks, but could neither find her nor learn what had become of her.

I had a friend and confidant, very near my own age, although appearing older, from his sprouting beard; he too was very fond of the ideal, and perhaps even more of a dreamer,—besides, he was the only person at the observatory with whom I was ever on intimate terms. He shared my joys and griefs. We had the same tastes, the same ideas, the same feelings. He understood my youthful admiration for the statue, the personality with which my imagination had invested her, and my unhappiness at having thus suddenly lost my dearest Urania just when I was most attached to her. He had more than once admired with me the effect of the light upon her celestial countenance, and smiled at my ecstasies like a big brother, even teasing me a little sharply about my affection for an idol, going so far as to call me "Camille Pygmalion." But at heart I knew that he too loved her.

This friend—who, alas! was to be torn from me a few years later, in the very flower of his youth, kind George Spero, exalted mind, noble heart, whose memory will be ever dear to me—was the director's private secretary; and his sincere affection for me was proved in this instance by an act of kindness as graceful as it was unexpected.

When I went home one day I saw with a half-incredulous bewilderment the famous clock standing on my chimney-piece there, just in front of me!

It was really she! How did she come there? What brought her there? Where did she come from?

I learned that the celebrated discoverer of Neptune had sent it to one of the principal clock-makers in Paris to be repaired; that the latter had received a most interesting antique astronomical clock from China and had offered it in exchange, which had been accepted; and that George Spero, to whom the transaction had been intrusted, had re-purchased Pradier's work as a gift for me. His parents were glad of an opportunity to please me, in remembrance of some lessons in mathematics which I had given George for his special examination.

What joy it was to see my Urania again! How happy I was to feast my eyes on her once more! That charming personification of the Muse of heaven has never left me since. In my studious hours the beautiful statue always stood before me, seeming to remind me of the goddess's conversation,—to tell me the destinies of astronomy, to direct me in my youthful scientific aspirations. Since then more passionate emotions have beguiled me, captivated me, and troubled my senses; but I shall never forget the ideal sentiment with which the Muse of the stars had inspired me, the celestial journey on which she bore me away, the unexpected panoramas she unrolled before my eyes, the truths she revealed to me as to the extent of the universe, nor the happiness she gave me by definitively settling my mind on the calm contemplation of Nature and science as a career.

Part Second.
—◆—
GEORGE SPERO.

I.
LIFE.

AN intense evening glow floated in the atmosphere like a wondrous golden radiance. From the heights of Passy the view extended over the whole of the great city, which at that time, more than ever before, was not a city, but a world. The Universal Exhibition of 1867 had lavished all the attractions and delights of the century on imperial Paris. The flowers of civilization were blooming in their most brilliant tints, wasting themselves away by the very ardor of their perfume,—fading, dying in the full fever of youth. The crowned heads of Europe had just heard a deafening trumpet-blast there, which was the last of the monarchy; science, arts, industry had sowed their newest creations broadcast, with an inexhaustible prodigality. It was a general delirium of men and things. Regiments were marching, with music at their heads; swift-rolling vehicles crossed each other from all directions; thousands of people were moving about in the dust on the avenues, *quais*, and boulevards: but the very dust, gilded by the rays of the setting sun, crowned the splendid city like an aureole. The tall buildings, towers, and steeples were ablaze with reflections from the fiery orb; tones from a distant orchestra, mingled with a confused murmur of voices and other sounds,—the brilliant, fit ending of a dazzling summer day,—poured into the soul an undefined feeling of contentment, happiness, and satisfaction. There was a kind of symbolical summing-up about it of the evidences of the vitality of a great people in the zenith of its life and fortune.

From the heights of Passy, where we are, on a terrace in a garden overhanging the careless current of the stream, as in the old days at Babylon, two persons, leaning on the stone balustrade, watch the noisy scene, looking down on the restless surface of the human sea, happier in their sweet solitude than all the atoms of that seething whirlpool; they do not belong to the every-day world, but soar above all that restless activity in the limpid atmosphere of their own joy. Their spirits feel, their hearts love; or to express the same fact more completely, their souls live.

In the maidenly beauty of her eighteenth spring, the young girl's glance wanders dreamily over the apotheosis of the setting sun. Happy to be alive, happier still to love, she gives no thought to the thousands of people moving about at her feet; she looks with unseeing eyes at the sun's ardent disk sinking below the purple western clouds; she breathes the perfumed air from garlands of roses in the garden, and feels through her whole being the peace of perfect happiness, singing a hymn of unutterable love in her heart. The blond hair waves about her brow like a misty aureole, and falls in thick tresses over her slender form; her blue eyes, fringed by long dark lashes, are like a reflection of the azure sky; her neck and arms give glimpses of the snowy whiteness of her skin; her cheeks, her ears, are softly colored; her whole person recalls somewhat the dainty marchionesses whom the painters of the eighteenth century loved to depict, who were born to an unknown life which they were not long destined to enjoy. She is standing. Her companion, whose arm a moment ago encircled her waist as they were looking at the picture of Paris and listening to the strains of melody flooding the air from the Imperial Guard, had seated himself by her side. His eyes had forgotten Paris and the setting sun; now they see nothing but the beautiful girl. He looks at her unconsciously with a strange, fixed gaze, as though he saw her now for the first time, and could not keep his eyes from her exquisite profile, enveloping her in a long look like a magnetic caress.

The young student was absorbed in his contemplation. Was he still a student at twenty-five? Is one ever anything more? And our own master then, M. de Chevreul, does he not call himself now, in his one hundred and third year, the senior of the students of France? George Spero had finished his lyceum studies at a very early age; but they teach nothing, unless it be how to work, and he continued to investigate the great problems of natural science with indefatigable ardor. Astronomy especially had at first attracted his interest. I had known him (as the reader of the first part of this book may remember) at the Paris Observatory, which he had entered at the age of sixteen, and where he had somewhat distinguished himself by a rather strange peculiarity,—that of having no ambition and no desire whatever for advancement.

At the age of sixteen, as at twenty-five, he believed himself to be on the verge of the grave,—judging, perhaps, that life indeed passes quickly, and that it is useless to wish for anything beyond the happiness of studying and knowing. He was not very talkative, although at heart his disposition was that of a playful child. His small, well-shaped mouth seemed to smile if one carefully examined its corners; otherwise it looked somewhat pensive, and as though made for silence. His eyes, whose undecided color reminded one of the bluish-green on the sea's horizon, changed with the light and in accordance with his moods; they were usually gentle, but on occasion would flash like lightning, or grow as cold as steel; their glance was deep, sometimes unfathomable, even strange and enigmatical. His ear was small, gracefully curved, the lobe well detached and a little raised,—which to analysts is an indication of refinement. The brow was broad, although his head was rather small, but seemed larger from his glistening, thickly waving hair; his beard was brown, like his hair, and slightly curled. Of medium height, his whole effect was elegant, with a natural ease; he dressed carefully, but without pretence or affectation.

My friends and I never had any special companionship with him. Holidays and leisure hours he never spent with us. Always occupied with his books, he seemed to have given himself up without reserve to hunting for the philosopher's stone, the quadrature of the circle, or perpetual motion. I never knew him to have a friend, unless it were myself; and yet I am not sure that he gave me all his confidences,—though, for that matter, perhaps there was no special event in his life except the one of which I now make myself the historian, and which I knew all about as an eye-witness if not as confidant.

The problem of the soul was the perpetual torment of his thought. Sometimes he was so absorbed in his search for the unknown, with such intense cerebral action, that he felt a sensation of tingling in his head which seemed to exhaust all his thinking faculties. This was especially the case when, after having analyzed the conditions of immortality for a long time, he saw real ephemeral life suddenly disappear, and endless immortality open before his mental being. In the face of this aspect of the soul in full eternity he longed *to know*. The sight of his own body, pale and stiff, wrapped in grave-clothes and lying in its coffin, left deserted in its last mournful resting-place at the bottom of a narrow grave under the grass where the cricket chirps, did not appall his thought so much as the uncertainty about the future. "What will become of me; what will become of us?" he repeated, like the constant clashing of a fixed idea in his brain. "If we die utterly, what an absurd farce life is, with its hopes and struggles. If we are immortal, what do we do with ourselves through endless eternity? Where shall I be a hundred years from now? Where will all the present dwellers of the earth be? To die, for ever and ever; to have existed but for a moment! What a mockery! Would it not be better a hundred times over never to have been born? But if it be our fate to live eternally and never to be able to change anything of the fatality that carries us along,—having endless eternity always before us,—how can we bear the burden of such a destiny? Is that the doom awaiting us? If we should tire of existence, we should be forbidden to fly from it; it would be impossible to end it. In this conception there is far more implacable cruelty than in that of an ephemeral life vanishing away like an insect's flight in the fresh evening breeze. Why then were we born? To suffer uncertainty; to find after examination not a single one of our hopes left; to live like idiots if we do not think, like fools if we do? And yet they tell us of a 'good God!' There are religions, priests, rabbis, bonzes. Why, mankind is but a race of dupes and duped! Religion is the same as patriotism, and the priest is as good as the soldier. Men of all nations arm themselves to the teeth that they may kill one another like simpletons! Ah! it is the wisest thing they could do; the best return they could make to Nature for the foolish gift she bestowed in causing them to be born."

I tried to lessen his pain and anxiety, having a certain philosophy of my own which was relatively satisfactory to me. "The fear of death seems absolutely chimerical," said I. "There are but two hypotheses to make about it: every night it may be that we shall not wake again the next morning; and yet, when we think of it, this idea does not prevent our going to sleep. Now, then, first, either all being ended with life, we do not wake again anywhere,—and in that case it is a sleep that has not ended, but which will endure throughout eternity, so that we shall never know anything about it,—or else, secondly, the soul outliving the body, we shall wake up somewhere else and continue our activity. In that case there is nothing to fear in the awakening,—it should rather attract us. There is a reason for all things in Nature; and every creature, the meanest as well as the noblest, finds his happiness in the exercise of his faculties."

This reasoning seemed to calm him; but the restlessness of doubt soon returned, pricking like thorns. Sometimes he would wander off alone through the spacious cemeteries of Paris, seeking out the most deserted alleys between the graves, listening to the wind among the trees, and the rustle of the leaves in the paths. Sometimes he went away into the woods in the suburbs of the great city, and would walk about for hours at a time muttering to himself. At other times he would spend a whole day in his study in the Place du Panthéon, which he used as study, work and reception room at the same time; and there, until far into the night, he would dissect a brain brought back from the clinic, studying the small slices of gray substance through his microscope.

The uncertainty of the sciences called positive, the sudden halt to his mind in the solution of these problems, threw him into fits of deepest despair; and I have found him many times in a state of utter prostration, his eyes set and shining, his hands burning with fever, his pulse agitated and intermittent. In one of these crises I was obliged to leave him for a few hours, and almost feared I should not find him alive on my return, at about five o'clock in the morning. He had near him a glass of cyanide of potassium, which he tried to hide as I came in; but recovering his calmness almost at once, he said, with great serenity and a slight smile, "What is the good? If we are immortal, it would be of no use, and I wanted to know about it sooner." That day he acknowledged he believed that he had been lifted painfully by his hair to the ceiling, and allowed to drop with all his weight upon the floor.

Public indifference with regard to the great problem of human destiny,—a question which in his eyes exceeded all others in importance, since it treated of our continued existence or destruction,—exasperated him to the last degree. All about him he saw people who were occupied solely by material interests, entirely absorbed by the foolish idea of "making money," for which they gave up all their years, their days, their hours, their minutes, disguised under various forms; and he found no free, independent mind living an intellectual life. It seemed to him that sentient beings could, *should*, while living the bodily life, since one cannot do otherwise, at least not remain the slaves of so coarse an organization, but devote the best moments to their intellectual life.

At the time this story begins, George Spero was already well known, and even famed, by the original scientific books which he had published, and also by several books of high literary merit, which had won praise for his name in all parts of the world.

Although he had not yet completed his twenty-fifth year, thousands of persons had read his books, which, however, were not written for the general public, but had been so successful as to be appreciated by the majority who desire to learn, as well as by the enlightened minority. He had been proclaimed master of a new school, and eminent critics, knowing neither his physical individuality nor his age, spoke of his "doctrines."

How did it happen that this philosopher of such rare ability, this stern student, should be at a young girl's feet at sunset on the terrace where we met them just now? The rest of the story will tell you.

II.
THE APPARITION.

THEIR first meeting had been a very strange one. The young naturalist was a passionate admirer of the beauties of Nature, and was always looking for grand effects. The year before, he had made a journey to Norway to visit the silent fiords, in which the sea was swallowed up; the mountains, whose snow-crowned summits lift their spotless brows far above the clouds; and to make a special study of the aurora borealis,—that most magnificent exhibition of our planet's life. I had accompanied him on the journey. The sunsets over the deep, calm fiords, the rise of the splendid orb on the mountains, charmed his poetic and artistic soul with an indescribable emotion. We remained there more than a month, going through the picturesque region of the Scandinavian Alps. Now, Norway was the home of that child of the North who was to exert so strong an influence over his unawakened heart. She was there, only a few steps away from him; and yet it was not until the very day we left that Chance, that god of the ancients, decided to bring them together.

The morning light was gilding the distant summits. The young Norwegian girl's father had brought her to one of the mountains much frequented by excursionists, like the Righi in Switzerland, to see the sunrise, which that day was of surpassing beauty. To better distinguish certain details of the landscape, Icléa had mounted a little hillock a few yards farther away, and was quite alone; when turning with her face from the sun to embrace the whole horizon, she saw her own image, her whole figure, not on the mountain nor the earth, but on the very sky itself. A luminous aureole framed her head and shoulders with a shining crown of glory, and a large aerial circle, faintly tinted with the colors of the rainbow, surrounded the mysterious apparition.

Astonished and touched by the singularity of the vision, and still under the influence of the gorgeous sunrise, she did not at first notice that another face, that of a man, was by the side of her own,—the motionless silhouette of a traveller in contemplation before her, recalling the statues of saints on their pedestals in churches. This masculine figure and her own were framed in by the same aerial circle. Suddenly she perceived the strange profile in the air, and thought herself the plaything of a fantastic vision; she started back in her amazement with a gesture of surprise, almost of fear. Her image in the air reproduced the same gesture, and she saw the traveller's wraith put his hand to his hat and take it off, as if he were bowing to the heavens, then lose the clearness of its outlines, and fade away at the same time as her own figure.

The transfiguration on Mount Tabor when the disciples of Jesus suddenly saw their Master's image on the sky, accompanied by those of Moses and Elias, could not have caused its witnesses any greater stupefaction than the innocent Norwegian girl felt before this *anthelion*, whose theory is well known to all meteorologists.

This apparition fixed itself upon her mental retina like a marvellous dream. She called her father, who had remained a few steps away from the little mound; but when he reached her it had all disappeared. She asked him to explain it; but he replied only by a doubt, almost a denial, of the truth of the phenomenon. The excellent man, formerly a field-officer, belonged to that category of distinguished sceptics who simply deny everything of which they are ignorant or which they cannot explain. It was all in vain that the lovely girl assured him that she had seen her reflection in the sky, and also that of a man whom she judged was young and good-looking; all in vain that she related the details of the apparition, and added that the figures were much larger than life-size, like enormous silhouettes,—he declared authoritatively and with considerable emphasis that it was what is called an optical illusion, produced by the imagination when one has not slept well, particularly in youth.

But on the evening of that day, as we were going on board the steamer, I noticed a young girl, with wind-tossed hair, who was looking at my friend in open astonishment. She had her father's arm, and was standing on the wharf as motionless as Lot's wife turned into a pillar of salt. I signed to my friend; but no sooner had he turned his head towards her than I saw her face crimson with a sudden flush: she at once turned away, and fixed her eyes on the paddle-wheel, which was just beginning to move. I do not know whether Spero noticed her confusion. As a fact, we had seen nothing of that morning's aerial phenomenon, at least not while the young girl was near us, and she had been hidden from us by a little clump of bushes; the magnificence of the sunrise had drawn us rather to the western side. However, he saluted Norway, which he regretted to leave, with the same gesture with which he had greeted the rising sun, and the pretty stranger had taken the bow for herself.

Two months later, the Comte de K—— gave a large reception in honor of the recent successes of his compatriot, Christine Nilsson. The young Norwegian girl and her father, who had come to Paris to pass a part of the winter, were among the guests, who had long known each other as fellow-countrymen, Norway and Sweden being sisters. We went there for the first time, our invitation being due to the appearance of Spero's latest book, which had already met with signal success. Icléa was a dreamy, thoughtful girl, well informed, thanks to the sound education given in Northern countries; she was eager to learn, and had read and re-read with curiosity the somewhat mystical book in which the new metaphysician, dissatisfied with Pascal's "Thoughts," had laid bare his soul's anxieties. Several months before, she had successfully passed the *brevet supérieur* examination; and having abandoned the study of medicine, which had at first attracted her, was beginning to look with some curiosity into the recent investigations of psychological physiology.

When M. George Spero was announced, she felt that an unknown friend, almost a confidant, had arrived. She started as if from an electric shock. He was not much of a society man. Timid, ill at ease in mixed assemblies, he did not care to dance, play, or converse, but preferred to stay apart in one corner of the room with some friends; quite indifferent to the waltzes and quadrilles, but more attentive to several masterpieces of modern music feelingly played. The entire evening passed without his being near her, although he had noticed her, and in all that brilliant ball had seen but her. Their eyes met many times. At last, about two o'clock in the morning, when the company was less formal, he ventured to approach her, without speaking, however. It was she who first spoke to him, to express a doubt about the conclusion of his last book.

Flattered, but still more surprised to learn that those metaphysical pages had had so young a reader, and a lady too, the author replied rather awkwardly that those investigations were somewhat uninteresting for a woman. She answered that women, and even young girls, were not exclusively absorbed in frivolity; that she knew several who occasionally worked, thought, endeavored, and studied. She spoke with a good deal of spirit, defending women against the contempt of certain scientists of the other sex, and maintained their intellectual equality. She had no trouble in winning a cause to which her listener was by no means hostile.

The new book—whose success had been immediate and brilliant, notwithstanding the gravity of its subject—had surrounded George Spero's name with an actual halo of fame, and the brilliant writer was warmly welcomed in every drawing-room. The two young people had exchanged but a few words when they found themselves the general object of attention, and were forced to reply to different questions, which interrupted their interview. One of the most eminent critics of the day had recently devoted a long article to the new work, and the subject of the book became at once the topic of general conversation. Icléa took no part in it; but she felt—and women are not often mistaken—that the hero had noticed her, that her thought was already linked to his by an invisible thread, and that while he replied to the more or less common-place questions thrust upon him, his mind was not wholly on the conversation. This first little triumph was enough, she cared for no other; and moreover she had recognized in his profile both the mysterious silhouette in the aerial apparition and the young stranger on the steamer at Christiania.

In that first interview he had not hesitated to express his enthusiastic admiration for the marvellous scenery in Norway, and to tell her about his visit there. She was eager for a word, some sort of an allusion to the aerial phenomenon which had made so great an impression upon her, and could not understand his silence in regard to it. Not having observed the *anthelion* when she was reflected upon it, he had not been particularly surprised at an occurrence which he had already studied before and under better conditions,—from the car of a balloon; and having seen nothing specially noticeable, had nothing to say about it. The occurrence at the steamboat landing too had entirely passed from his memory; so that although the fair beauty of the young girl did not seem entirely unfamiliar to him, yet he had no recollection of having met her before. As for me, I had recognized her at once. He talked about the lakes, rivers, fiords, and mountains of Norway; learned from her that her mother had died very young from heart-disease, that her father preferred living in Paris to anywhere else, and that it was probable she should not visit her native land except at rare intervals for the future.

A remarkable identity of ideas and tastes, a ready and mutual sympathy, a reciprocal respect, soon made them friends. Brought up and educated with English ideas, she enjoyed that independence of mind and freedom of action which Frenchwomen never know until after marriage; she felt hampered by none of the social conventionalities which with us are supposed to protect innocence and virtue. Two friends of her own age had even come to Paris to finish their musical education. They were living together in the very heart of Babylon in perfect safety, never even suspecting the dangers by which Paris is said to be beset. The young girl received George Spero's visits as her father would have received them himself; and in a few weeks the congeniality in their tastes and dispositions had united them in the same studies, the same researches, often in the very same thoughts. Almost every afternoon he went, drawn by a secret attraction, from the Latin quarter along the borders of the Seine as far as the Trocadéro, and passed several hours with Icléa either in the library, on the garden-terrace, or walking in the wood.

The first impression aroused by the apparition on the sky had remained in Icléa's mind. She looked up to the young savant, if not as a god or hero, at least as a man far superior to his contemporaries. The perusal of his works strengthened this feeling and increased it; she felt more than admiration, she had an actual veneration for him. When she knew him personally, the great man did not descend from his pedestal. She found him so high, so excellent in his works, his inquiries, his studies, and at the same time so simple, so sincere, so good-natured, so indulgent to all, and (seizing any pretext for hearing him talked about), she was sometimes forced to listen to such unjust criticisms upon him from rivals, that she began to have an almost maternal feeling for him. Does the sentiment of protecting affection exist in every young girl's heart? Perhaps. But assuredly she loved him thus at first. I have already said that the basis of this thinker's character was somewhat melancholy,—that melancholy of the soul of which Pascal speaks, and which is like homesickness for heaven. In fact, he was ever seeking to solve the eternal question, Hamlet's "To be, or not to be?" Sometimes he would be sad, downcast. But by a singular contrast, when his unhappy thoughts had worn themselves out, so to speak, in vain research, and his exhausted brain had lost the power of further vibration, a kind of repose came to him,—he recovered his ordinary quiet; the circulation of his red blood stimulated his organic life; philosophy disappeared, leaving him like a simple child, amused at trifles; and having almost feminine tastes, delighting in flowers, perfumes, music, revery, he appeared sometimes astonishingly light-hearted.

III.
"TO BE, OR NOT TO BE?"

IT was this very phase of his intellectual life which had drawn the two friends so intimately together. Happy at being alive, in the flower of her spring-time, expanding to the light of life,—a harp thrilling with all the harmonies of Nature,—the beautiful Northern girl still sometimes dreamed of the fays and elves of her native clime, of the angels and mysteries of the Christian religion which had soothed her childhood. The credulity of her early days had not obscured her understanding; she thought freely, and sought sincerely for the truth; while regretting perhaps that she no longer believed in the paradise of the preachers, she felt nevertheless a strong desire to live forever. Death seemed to her a cruel injustice. She never thought of her mother lying on her death-bed in the ripe beauty of her thirtieth year,—taken away to the green and fragrant cemetery, filled with the songs of birds, while the roses were in full bloom; crossed off the book of life while all Nature still sang, still bloomed and shone,—she never thought of her mother's pale face, as I said, without a sudden shudder creeping all over her from head to foot. No, her mother was not dead! She would not die at thirty, or at any time! And he? He die! That sublime mind to be blotted out by a stoppage of the heart or breath? No, it was not possible! Men are mistaken! We shall know some day!

Then, too, sometimes she thought of these mysteries under a form rather more æsthetic and sentimental than scientific; but she thought of them. All her questionings, her doubts, the secret object of her conversations, perhaps her rapidly developed attachment for her friend,—the cause of it all was the insatiable thirst for knowledge which consumed her soul. She hoped in him because she had already found in his writings a solution to the highest problems. He had taught her to know the universe; and she found this knowledge more beautiful, more vivid, more poetic, grander, than the old errors and illusions. From the time when he told her that life had no object other than the search for truth, she had felt sure that he would find it; and her mind clung to and bound itself to his even more strongly than her heart.

They had lived a common intellectual life in this way for about three months, almost every day spending several hours reading original essays, written in different languages, on science and philosophy,—the theory of atoms, molecular physics, organic chemistry, thermo-dynamics, and the different sciences whose object is the knowledge of existence,—or in discoursing upon the real or apparent contradictions of hypotheses; sometimes finding statements and coincidences most remarkable for their scientific axioms, in the books of purely literary writers, and occasionally astonished at the foresight of some great authors. These readings, investigations, and comparisons had especially interested them by the discrimination which their minds were led to make, as they became more and more enlightened, between nine tenths of the writers whose works are absolutely worthless, and half of the last tenth, whose writings have but a superficial value. Having thus cleared the field of literature, they took great delight and satisfaction in the restricted society of superior minds. Perhaps mixed with it was a little feeling of pride.

One day Spero arrived earlier than usual. "Eureka!" he cried. But correcting himself quickly, added, "Perhaps."

Leaning against the chimney-piece, where a bright fire crackled, while his companion looked at him with her large eyes full of curiosity, he began to speak with a sort of unconscious solemnity, as though he were discussing something with his own mind in the solitude of the woods.

*****

"What we see is only apparent. Reality is quite different.

"The sun apparently turns about us, rising every morning, setting at night; the earth where we are seems to be motionless: but the contrary is the truth. We live on a whirling projectile, thrown into space with a speed seventy-five times as great as that which carries a cannon-ball.

"Our ears are pleased by a harmonious concert. Sound does not exist; it is merely an impression of the senses produced by vibrations of a certain size and rapidity on the air, which in themselves are silent. There would be no sound without the acoustic nerve and the brain. In reality there is nothing but motion.

"The rainbow spreads its radiant circle; the rose and corn-flower, dripping with rain, glitter in the sun; the green meadow, the golden furrow, diversify the plain with their bright colors. There are no colors; there is no light,—there is nothing but the ether waves, which cause a vibration of the optic nerve. Appearances are deceitful. The sun warms and fertilizes; fire burns. There is no heat, only sensation; heat, like light, is but one form of motion,—invisible but supreme, sovereign motion!

*****

"Take a strong iron beam, like one of those used so generally in building nowadays. It is set up in space, ten metres high, between two walls which support its ends. It is 'solid.' In the middle of it is placed a weight of one, two, or ten thousand kilograms; but it does not even show this enormous weight,—a level would hardly find a depression in it. And yet this beam is composed of particles which do not touch each other, which are in perpetual vibration, which separate under the influence of heat, and are drawn together by cold. Tell me, if you please, in what the solidity of this bar of iron consists. Its material atoms? Assuredly not, since they do not touch. That solidity lies in molecular attraction,—that is to say, in an immaterial force.

"Speaking absolutely, solidity does not exist. Take up a heavy iron cannon-ball: this ball is composed of invisible molecules which do not touch each other. The continuity which the surface seems to have, and the apparent solidity of the ball are, then, pure illusions. To the mind which would analyze it, its inner structure is an eddying swarm of little gnats, like those darting about in the air on a summer day. Then suppose we heat this apparently solid ball: it will melt; heat it more, it will evaporate,—but without changing its nature for all that; gas or liquid, it will still be iron.

"We are in a house. All these walls, these floors, these carpets, this furniture, the marble mantelpiece, are also composed of particles which do not touch each other; and all these particles which constitute these objects are in constant motion, circulating around each other.

"Our body is in the same condition. It is formed by a perpetual circulation of molecules; it is a flame which is ceaselessly consumed and renewed; it is a stream on whose banks one sits down, expecting to see the same water again, but the perpetual course of things always brings fresh water. Each globule of our blood is a world (and we have five millions per cubic millimetre). Constantly, without let or hindrance, in our arteries and veins, in our flesh, in our brain, all circulates,—all moves, all hurries along in a vital whirl as rapid, proportionately, as that of the heavenly bodies. Molecule by molecule, our brain, our skull, our eyes, our nerves, our entire flesh ceaselessly renews itself, and so rapidly that in a few months our entire body is reconstituted.

*****

"From estimates founded on molecular attraction it has been calculated that in a tiny drop of water taken up on the point of a pin, a drop invisible to the naked eye, measuring one thousandth of a cubic millimetre, there are more than two hundred and twenty-five million molecules.

"In the head of a pin there are not less than eight sextillions of atoms, or eight thousand millions of millions of millions; and these atoms are separated from each other by distances greater than their dimensions, these dimensions being invisible even to the most powerful microscope. If one felt inclined to count the number of these atoms contained in the head of a pin, by detaching in thought a thousand million of them per second, it would be necessary to continue the operation for two hundred and fifty-three thousand years, in order to finish the enumeration.

"In a drop of water, in the head of a pin, there are incomparably more atoms than there are stars in all the sky known to astronomers, armed with their strongest telescopes.

*****

"What upholds the earth, the sun, and all the stars of the universe in the eternal void? What upholds that heavy iron beam thrown between two walls, and upon which several stories are to be built? What keeps all bodies in shape? Force.

"The world, beings, and things, all that we see, is formed of invisible and imponderable atoms. The universe is a dynamism. God is the universal soul; *in eo vivimus, movemur, et sumus.*

"As the soul is force moving the body, the Infinite Being is force moving the universe. The purely mechanical theory is incomplete to an analyst who goes to the bottom of things. It is true that the human *will* is weak, in comparison to cosmic forces; yet by sending a train from Paris to Marseilles, a ship from Marseilles to Suez, I freely displace an infinitesimal portion of the earth's matter, and modify the moon's course. Blind men of the nineteenth century, come back to the swan of Mantua: *Mens agitat molem.*

"If I dissect matter, I find the invisible atom at the base of everything. Matter disappears, fades away into smoke. If my eyes had power enough to see the truth, they would see, through walls and bodies composed of separate molecules, atomic swarms. The eyes of the flesh do not see what is. The mind's eye must see. Do not rely on the evidence of your senses alone; there are as many stars over our heads in the daytime as there are during the night.

"In Nature there is neither astronomy nor chemistry nor philosophy nor mechanics; those are subjective methods of observation. There is but a single unit. The infinitely great is identical with the infinitely small. Space is infinite without being great. Time is eternal without being long. Stars and atoms are one.

*****

"The unity of the universe is constituted of invisible, imponderable, immaterial force, which moves atoms. If a single atom should cease to be moved by force, the universe would stop. The earth turns round the sun, the sun gravitates around a sidereal arch, which is itself capable of motion; the millions, the thousand millions of suns which people the universe move much more rapidly than gunpowder projectiles; these stars which seem to us to be motionless are suns thrown into the eternal void at the speed of ten, twenty, thirty millions of kilometres a day, all rushing towards an unknown goal,—suns, planets, earths, satellites, wandering comets ...; the fixed point, the centre of gravity sought after by analysts, flies as fast as it is pursued, and really exists nowhere. The atoms of which bodies are composed, move relatively as fast as stars in the sky. Motion regulates all things, forms all things.

"*The atom itself is not an inert mass, it is a centre of force.*

"That which essentially constitutes and organizes the human being, is not his material substance; it is not the protoplasm, nor the cell, nor those marvellous and fertile combinations of carbon with hydrogen, oxygen, and nitrogen,—it is animate, invisible, immaterial *Force*. It is that which groups, directs, and keeps together the innumerable particles which compose the exquisite harmony of the living body.

"Matter and energy have never been seen separated from each other; the existence of one implies the existence of the other; they are perhaps substantially identical.

"If the body should suddenly decay after death, as it slowly disintegrates and perpetually renews itself during life, it would matter little. The soul remains. *The organizing cerebral atom is the centre of this force.* It also is indestructible.

"What we see is deceitful. *The real is the invisible.*"

*****

He began to pace up and down the floor. The young girl had listened to him as one listens to an apostle, a loved apostle; and although he had really spoken but for her, he had not apparently realized her presence,—she had been so silent and motionless. She went to him and took one of his hands in hers. "Oh!" she cried, "if you have not yet conquered Truth, she cannot elude you."

Then, growing excited herself, and alluding to an often-expressed reservation of his, "You think," she added, "that it is impossible for terrestrial man to attain to the truth because we have but five senses, and that a multitude of natural manifestations are unknown to our minds because we have no means of reaching them. Just as sight would be denied us if we were deprived of the optic nerve, hearing if we had no acoustic nerve, etc.; just as the vibrations, the exhibitions of force which pass between the strings of our organic instrument, without causing those we have to quiver, are unknown to us. I concede that, and agree with you that the inhabitants of certain worlds maybe incomparably more advanced than we; but it seems to me that although earthly, you have found it out."

"My darling," he answered, sitting down beside her on the wide library lounge, "it is very certain that some of the strings in our terrestrial harp are missing: probably a citizen of the Sirius system would laugh at our pretentions. The smallest piece of magnetized iron is stronger in finding the magnetic pole than either Newton or Leibnitz, and the swallow knows the variations of latitude better than did Christopher Columbus or Magellan. What did I say just now? That appearances are deceitful, and that our minds must see invisible force through matter. That is perfectly sure. Matter is not what it seems to be, and no man informed about the progress of the positive sciences could now pretend to be a materialist."

"Then," she said, "the cerebral atom, the principle of human organism, would be immortal, like all other atoms, if one should admit the fundamental assertions of chemistry. But it would differ from the others, possessing a higher rank, the soul being attached to it. And would it preserve the consciousness of its existence? Would the soul be comparable to an electric substance? Once I saw the lightning go through a drawing-room and extinguish the lights; when they were re-lighted, we found that the gilding had all been taken off the clock, and that the chased silver candlestick was gilded in several places. That is a subtle force!"

"Do not draw comparisons; they would be too far from the truth. There is no doubt that the soul exists, as force does. We can admit that it and the cerebral atom are one; that it thus survives the dissolution of the body we can imagine."

"But what becomes of it? Where does it go?"

"The greater number of souls never even suspect their own existence. Out of the fourteen hundred millions of human beings who people the earth, ninety-nine one hundredths do not think. Great heavens! what would they do with immortality? As the molecule of iron floats in the blood, throbbing in Lamartine's or Hugo's temple, or is fixed for a time in Cæsar's sword; as the molecule of hydrogen shines in the lobby of a theatre, or merges itself into the drop of water swallowed by a fish in the dusky depths of the sea, so living atoms sleep which have never thought. Thinking souls are the inheritance of the intellectual life. They preserve humanity's patrimony, and increase it for the future. Without this immortality of human souls which are conscious of their existence and live through the mind, all the history of the earth would end in nothing, and the whole creation, that of the most sublime worlds as well as that of our mean little planet, would be a deceptive absurdity, more miserable and pitiable than the cast of an earthworm. That has a right to be; but the universe would not have. Do you imagine that the thousand millions of worlds attain the splendors of life and thought, to succeed each other without end in the sidereal universe, only to give birth to constantly deceived hopes, and grandeurs which are perpetually destroyed? It is useless for us to humble ourselves; we cannot admit that nothing is the supreme object of perpetual progress, proved by all the history of Nature. Now, souls are the seeds of planetary humanities."

"Can they transport themselves from one world to another?"

"Nothing is so difficult to understand as that of which one is ignorant, nothing more simple than what one knows. Who is surprised now to see that the electric telegraph instantly sends human thought across continents and seas? Who is surprised to see lunar attraction raise the waters of the ocean and produce tides? Who is surprised to see light transmit itself from one star to another at the rate of three hundred thousand kilometres per second? Besides, thinkers alone could appreciate the grandeur of these marvels; the vulgar are surprised at nothing. If some new discovery to-morrow should enable us to make signals to the inhabitants of Mars and receive replies from them, three quarters of mankind would think nothing of it the day after. Yes, the animating forces can transport themselves from one world to the other; not everywhere nor always, to be sure, and not all of them. There are laws and conditions. My will, with the help of my muscles, can raise my arm or throw a stone; if I take a weight of twenty kilos, it will still raise my arm; if I want to raise a weight of a thousand kilos, I can no longer do it. Some minds are incapable of any activity; others have acquired transcendent faculties. Mozart at six years of age surprised all his hearers by the power of his musical genius, and at eight published his first two sonatas; while the greatest dramatic author who ever existed, Shakspeare, had written nothing worthy of his name until after he was thirty years old. It is not necessary to believe that the soul should belong to some supernatural world. Everything is in Nature. It is hardly more than a hundred thousand years since terrestrial humanity evolved itself from the animal chrysalis. For millions of years, during the long historic series of the primary, secondary, and tertiary periods, there was not a single eye on the earth to see these grand sights, a single human mind to contemplate them. Progress has slowly raised the inferior souls of plants and animals; man is quite recent on the planet. Nature is in ceaseless progress, the universe is a perpetual growth, ascent is the supreme law.

"All worlds," he added, "are not actually inhabited. Some are at the dawn, others at twilight. For example, in our solar system, Mars, Venus, Saturn, and several of his satellites seem to be in full vital activity. Jupiter appears not to have passed its primary period; the Moon has perhaps no longer any inhabitants. Our own period is of no more importance in the general history of the universe than one anthill in the infinite. Before the existence of the earth, there had been, from all eternity, worlds peopled with humanities. When our planet shall have ceased to live, and the last human family shall have fallen asleep on the brink of the last lagoon of the frozen ocean, numberless suns will still shine in the infinite, there will still be mornings and evenings, spring-time and flowers, hopes and joys, other suns, other earths, other humanities,—boundless space, peopled with tombs and cradles. But life, thought, eternal progress, are the final object of creation.

"The earth is a star's satellite. Now, as well as in the future, we are citizens of the sky; whether we know it or not, we are really living in the stars."

Thus the two friends conversed about the deep subjects which engrossed their thoughts; when they were conquering a problem, even if it were incomplete, they experienced a true happiness at having taken another step in their search for the unknown, and could then talk more quietly about the ordinary things of life. They were two minds equally eager for knowledge, imagining in their youthful fervor that they could isolate themselves from the world, look down upon human ideas, and in their celestial flight reach the star of Truth, which shone above their heads in the depths of the infinite.

IV.
AMOR.

IN their life together, pleasant and intimate as it was, there was something lacking. These conversations on the serious topics of being or non-being, their exchange of ideas on the analysis of humanity, their inquiries into the final end of the existence of things, satisfied their minds sometimes, but not their hearts. When they had been together for a long time, talking under the garden trellis which towered above the picture of the great city, or in the silent library, the student, the thinker could not leave his companion; they sat hand in hand, mute, attracted and repelled by an irresistible power. After leaving each other, both felt a singular, painful void in their breasts, an indefinable uneasiness, as though some link necessary for both their lives had been broken; and each hoped for nothing but the hour of meeting. He loved her, not for himself, but for herself, with an almost impersonal affection, with a feeling of high esteem as well as ardent love; and by a constantly fought combat with his desire he had been able to resist it. But one day, when they were both sitting on the wide divan in the library, strewn, as usual, with books and loose leaves, a silence fell upon them, and it happened that, overcome perhaps by the weight of his long-continued efforts to resist so powerful an attraction, the young author's head insensibly drooped to his companion's shoulder, and almost at once ... their lips met....

Oh, unutterable joys of requited love; insatiable intoxication of the heart transported with happiness; never-ending delights of the uncurbed imagination; sweet music of the heart,—to what ethereal heights have you not raised the chosen ones, given up to your supreme felicities! Suddenly forgetful of this lower world, they fly on outstretched wings to some enchanted paradise, lose themselves in celestial depths, and soar away to the sublime regions of eternal rapture. The world, with its joys and its sorrows, no longer exists for them; they live in light, in fire,—they are salamanders, phœnixes, freed from all weight, light as flame, burning themselves out, rising again from their ashes, always luminous, always ardent, invulnerable, invincible.

The expansion of their first long-repressed delights threw the lovers into an ecstatic existence in which metaphysics and its problems were for a time forgotten. This lasted six months. The sweetest but most imperious of feelings had suddenly absorbed and taken possession of them, thus completing the insufficient intellectual satisfactions of the mind. From the day of the kiss, George Spero not only entirely disappeared from society, but even ceased to write; and I lost sight of him myself, notwithstanding the long and true affection he had professed for me. Logicians might have been able to conclude from this that for the first time in his life he was satisfied that he had found the solution of the great problem,—the supreme object of the existence of beings.

They were living in this "selfishness for two" which, while moving mankind from our optic centre, diminishes its defects and makes it appear more beautiful. Satisfied by their mutual affection, everything in nature and humanity sang a perpetual hymn of happiness and love. Often in the evening they walked along the banks of the Seine, dreamily contemplating the effects of light and shade which make the sky of Paris so exquisite at twilight, when the silhouettes of towers and buildings are thrown out against the luminous background in the west. Piles of rose-colored and purple clouds, illuminated by the distant reflection of the sea over which the vanished sun is still shining, give our skies a character of their own, not like that of Naples, bathed in the west by the Mediterranean mirror, but surpassing Venice perhaps, whose illumination is pale and eastern. It might chance that, their steps having led them to the old island of the Cité, they would stroll along the river bank, passing in sight of Notre Dame and the old Châtelet, whose dark outlines might still be seen against the dimly lighted sky. Sometimes, often indeed, enticed by the brilliance of the setting sun and by the fresh green of the country, they went along the *quais*, out beyond the ramparts of the great city, and strayed as far as the solitudes of Boulogne or Billancourt, shut in between the dusky hills of Meudon and Saint-Cloud. They were contemplating Nature; they forgot the noisy city lost behind them; and walking with the same step, forming but one being, they received the same impressions, thought the same thoughts, and by their silence spoke the same language.

The stream flowed on at their feet, the noises of the day were dying away, the first stars were peeping out. Icléa liked to tell George their names as they appeared.

March and April often offer Paris mild evenings, on which the first warm breezes, forerunners of spring, greet us. Orion's brilliant stars, the dazzling Sirius, the Twins, Castor and Pollux glitter in the immense sky; the Pleiades sink towards the western horizon; but Arcturus and Boötes, shepherd of the celestial flocks, return, and a few hours later white and resplendent Vega rises on the eastern horizon, soon followed by the Milky Way. Arcturus with its golden rays is always the first star to be recognized, from its piercing brilliancy and from its position in the prolongation of the tail of the Great Bear. Sometimes the lunar crescent was hanging in the western sky, and the young girl gazed admiringly, like Ruth by Boaz' side, at "that golden sickle in the field of stars."

The stars surround the earth, the earth is in the sky. Spero and his companion realized this, and perhaps no other couple on any other celestial earth lived on more intimate terms than they with the sky and infinity.

And yet by degrees, perhaps without noticing it himself, the young philosopher was gradually taking up again by shattered fragments his interrupted studies; analyzing subjects now with a deep feeling of optimism which he had never known before, in spite of his natural kindliness; excluding cruel conclusions because they seemed to him to be due to an insufficient knowledge of causes, looking at the panoramas of Nature and of humanity in a new light. She too had taken up, at least partially, the studies which she had begun in common with him; but a new feeling filled her soul, and her mind had not the same freedom for intellectual work. Absorbed in this constant affection for a being whom she had wholly won, she saw only through him, acted only by him. In quiet evening hours, when she went to the piano and played a sonata by Chopin, which she was astonished to find she had not understood until she was in love, or to accompany her pure rich voice while singing the Norwegian *lieder* by Grieg or Bull, or our own Gounod's melodies, it seemed to her, unconsciously perhaps, that her lover was the only listener capable of appreciating these inspirations of the heart. What delicious hours he spent, stretched on a divan in that spacious library in the house at Passy, sometimes idly following the capricious rings of smoke from a Turkish cigarette, while she gave herself up to fanciful memories, singing the sweet *Saetergientens Sondag* of her native land, the serenade from "Don Juan," Lamartine's "Lake," or else when running her skilful fingers over the keys she sent the melodious dream of Boccherini's minuet floating into the air.

Spring had come. May had brought the opening fêtes at the Universal Exhibition of which we spoke at the beginning of this story, and the great trees in the garden at Passy shaded the Eden of the loving couple. Icléa's father, who had suddenly been called to Tunis, returned with a collection of Arabian arms for his museum at Christiania. He intended to go back to Norway very soon, and it had been agreed between the young Norwegian girl and her lover that the marriage should take place in her native land on the anniversary of the mysterious apparition.

Their love was, from its very nature, very far removed from all those common-place unions founded, some on gross sensual pleasure, others on motives of interest more or less disguised, which represent the greater part of human love. Their cultivated minds kept them isolated in the loftier regions of thought; their delicacy of feeling kept them in an ideal atmosphere where all material burdens were forgotten; the extreme impressibility of their nerves, the exquisite refinement of all their sensations, brought them delights whose enjoyment seemed to have no end. If there is love in other worlds, it can be no deeper or more exquisite feeling. To a physiologist they would have been the living witnesses of the fact that, contrary to ordinary opinion, all enjoyment comes from the brain, the intensity of sensation corresponding to the psychic sensibility of the being.

Paris was for them, not a city, not a world, but the theatre of human history. They lived the past centuries over again. The old quarters which had not yet been ruined by modern changes,—the Cité, with Notre Dame, Saint-Julien le Pauvre, whose walls still recall Chilpéric and Frédégonde; the old houses where Albert le Grand, Petrarch, Dante, Abelard, had lived; the old University, anterior to the Sorbonne, and belonging to the same vanished centuries; the cloister of Saint-Merry with its sombre little paths, the abbey of Saint-Martin, Clovis' tower on the mountain, Saint-Geneviève, Saint-Germain-des-Prés, a relic of the Merovingians, Saint-Germain-l'Auxerrois, whose bell sounded the tocsin, the Sainte-Chapelle at Louis IX.'s palace, all memorials of French history, were the object of their pilgrimages. They were alone in crowds, looking into the past and seeing what very few people know how to see.

And so the immense city spoke its language of other days,—either when, lost amid the monsters, griffins, pillars, and capitals, the arabesques of the tower and galleries of Notre Dame, they saw the human hive go to sleep at their feet in the evening dusk, or, when rising higher still, they tried from the top of the Panthéon to restore the old outlines of Paris and its gradual development from the Roman emperors who lived in the Baths, to Philip Augustus and his successors.

The spring sunshine, the blooming lilacs, the joyous May mornings, full of bird-songs and nervous exhilaration, often drew them at random away from Paris into the meadows and woods. The hours flew by like a breath of wind, the day had passed like a thought, and the night prolonged the divine dream of love. In the swiftly revolving world of Jupiter, where the days and nights are twice as rapid as they are here, and do not even last ten hours, lovers do not find the time fade away any more quickly. The measure of time is in ourselves.

They were sitting one evening on the roof of the old tower at the Château de Chevreuse; there was no railing, and they were close together in the centre, from whence one can look down over the unobstructed surrounding landscape. The warm air from the valley, impregnated with wild perfumes from the neighboring woods, rose to where they sat; the warbler was still singing, and the nightingale in the growing shadows was trying over his melodious hymn to the stars. The sun had just set in a blaze of crimson and gold, and the west alone was still illuminated by a glowing radiance. Everything seemed to be asleep on Nature's broad bosom.

Icléa was a little pale; but in the glow of the western sky her skin was so clear, so delicate, so ideal that the light seemed to penetrate it and illuminate it from within. Her eyes were misty with soft languor, and her little, childlike mouth was lightly parted; she seemed lost in contemplation of the sunset light. Leaning on Spero's breast, her arms twined about his neck, she was sinking into a revery when a shooting-star crossed the sky just over the tower. She started with a little feeling of superstition.

The most brilliant stars were already sparkling in the heavenly depths. Arcturus, a brilliant golden yellow, was very high, almost at the zenith; Vega, a pure white light, had already risen towards the west; in the north, Capella; in the west, Castor, Pollux, and Procyon. The seven stars of the Great Bear, Regulus, Spica Virginis, were also discernible. Noiselessly, one by one, the stars came out to punctuate the heavens. The north star showed the only motionless spot in the celestial sphere.

The moon was rising, its reddish disk somewhat diminished from being on the wane. Mars was shining between Pollux and Regulus in the southwest, Saturn in the southeast. Twilight was slowly yielding its place to the mysterious reign of night.

"Does it not seem to you," she asked, "that all these stars are like eyes looking down at us?"

"Celestial eyes, like yours. What can they see on earth more beautiful than you—and our love?"

"And yet—" she added.

"Yes, 'and yet,'—the world, family, society, custom, moral laws, and all that. I understand your thought. We have forgotten all these things to obey attraction alone,—like the sun, like all those stars, like the warbling nightingale, like all Nature. Very soon we shall give those social customs the part which belongs to them, and can openly proclaim our love. Shall we be any happier for that? Is it possible to be any happier than we are at this very moment?"

"I am yours," she replied, "I do not exist for myself. I am swallowed up in your light, your love, in your happiness, and I care for nothing, nothing more. No. I was thinking of those stars, of those eyes looking down at us, and wondering where all the human eyes are which have watched them for millions of years as we do to-night. Where are all the hearts that have beaten as our heart beats now? Where are all the souls who have lost themselves in endless kisses in the mysterious vanished nights?"

"They all exist, nothing can be destroyed. We associate heaven and earth, and we are right. In all the ages, with all peoples, among all beliefs, mankind has always asked the secret of its destiny of the starry heavens. That was one kind of divination. The Earth is a star of heaven, like Mars and Saturn, which we see yonder, earths of the sky, lighted by the same sun as we are, and like all these stars, which are distant suns. Thought translates what man has believed ever since it existed. All eyes have sought the answer to the great enigma in the skies, and Urania has replied to them since the early days of mythology."

The night was coming on. The moon, slowly rising in the eastern sky, was shedding her radiance through the atmosphere, insensibly displacing the twilight; and in the city at their feet, below the thickets and ruins, a few lights were already beginning to appear here and there. The two had risen, and were standing in the centre of the tower roof, closely clasped together. She was beautiful, framed in the aureole of her hair, whose curls floated over her shoulders; little puffs of spring-like air, fragrant with perfume of violets, gillyflowers, lilacs, and May roses were rising from the neighboring gardens. Solitude and silence were about them. Their lips united in a long kiss,—the hundredth at least of that beautiful day of spring. She was still dreaming. A fugitive smile suddenly lighted up her face, then faded away like a passing cloud.

"Of what are you thinking?" he asked.

"Oh, nothing! A worldly, foolish thought; a little silly—nothing."

"But what was it?" he asked, taking her again in his arms.

"Oh! I was only wondering if people had mouths in those other worlds; because, you know—a kiss—lips—"

And so the hours passed away,—days, weeks, months, in a perfect union of all their thoughts, all their feelings and impressions. The June sun was already shining at its solstice, and the time to leave for Icléa's home had come. At the appointed time she left with her father for Christiania, and Spero followed them a few days later. It was the young savant's intention to stay in Norway until autumn, and continue the studies on the aurora borealis he had begun the year before,—observations which were especially interesting to him, and which he had had scarcely time to begin.

This visit to Norway was the prolongation of a happy dream. The fair Northern girl cast an aureole of perpetual winsomeness about him which would perhaps have made him still forget the attractions of science if she herself had not had, as we have seen, an insatiable taste for study. The experiments which the indefatigable seeker had undertaken on atmospheric electricity interested her as much as they did him. She too wanted to know about those mysterious flames in the aurora borealis which palpitate at night in high atmospheres; and as his series of investigations led him to desire a balloon ascension, in order to reach and surprise the phenomenon at its source, she also experienced the same wish. He tried to dissuade her from it, those aeronautic expeditions not being free from danger. But the very idea of sharing a peril with him would have been enough to make her deaf to her loved one's entreaties. After long hesitation Spero decided to take her with him, and prepared for an ascension from the University of Christiania on the first night of the aurora borealis.

V.
THE AURORA BOREALIS.

THE disturbances of the magnetic needle had announced the aurora's presence even before the sun went down, and the inflation of the balloon with pure hydrogen gas was begun while the sky showed in the magnetic North that coloring of golden green which is always the sure indication of an aurora borealis. The preparations were ended in a couple of hours. The atmosphere, entirely free from all clouds, was perfectly limpid, the stars twinkled in the bosom of a sky profoundly dark and without a moon; but towards the North a soft light shone in an arc above a black segment, throwing into the upper atmosphere slight flushes of a pale greenish rose color, symbolizing the palpitations of an unknown life. Icléa's father, who was watching the inflation of the balloon, had no suspicion that his daughter was going; but at the last moment she stepped into the car as if to inspect it. Spero gave the signal, and the balloon rose slowly, majestically, over the city of Christiania, which, lighted by thousands of lamps, appeared under the eyes of the travellers rising through the air, to diminish in size as it disappeared in the darkness.

Soon the balloon, taking an oblique ascent, hovered over the darkened landscape, and the paling lights also disappeared. The noises of the city died away at the same time into profound silence: it was the silence of the upper heights which enveloped the air-ship now. Icléa was impressed by this extraordinary stillness, perhaps, above all, by the novelty of the situation, and clung to her rash lover's side. They mounted rapidly. The aurora borealis appeared to descend, and spread itself out under the stars, like an undulating drapery of fleecy gold and purple, overrun with electric flashes. Spero watched his instruments, and by the help of a little crystal globe filled with glow-worms, wrote down the indications corresponding to the heights attained. The balloon went up steadily. What a delight to the investigator! In a few moments he would soar to the crest of the aurora borealis; he would find an answer to the question about the aurora's height which had been asked in vain by so many philosophers, and especially by his beloved masters, the two great "psychologists and philosophers," Oersted and Ampère!

Icléa's emotion had calmed itself. "Were you afraid?" asked her lover. "The balloon is safe; you need fear no accident,—everything has been provided for. We will go down in an hour; there is not a breath of wind stirring on the earth."

"No," she said, while the celestial light threw over her a roseate and transparent illumination; "but it is so strange, so beautiful, so divine. It is grand for little me! I shuddered for a moment. It seems to me that I love you more than ever!" and throwing her arms about his neck, she kissed him in a long, passionate, clinging embrace.

The solitary balloon was moving silently through the aerial heights, a spheroid of transparent gas enclosed in its silken envelope, whose vertical gores, joining each other at the valve on the top, could be seen from the car; the lower part of the balloon being open for the dilation of the gas.

The dusky brightness that falls from the stars, of which Corneille speaks, would have been sufficient without the gleams from the aurora borealis to enable them to distinguish the whole of the aerial skiff. The car was hung to the net which enveloped the silken vessel by strong ropes tied to the basket-work and interlaced under the feet of the aeronauts. The silence was impressively solemn; the beating of their hearts could have been heard. They were sailing at a height of five thousand metres, with an unaccustomed gravity; the upper wind was carrying them along without the faintest breath being felt in the car, for the balloon floated in the moving air like a simple bubble,—motionless, except as the current carried it along. Our travellers—sole inhabitants of these lofty regions, in full enjoyment of the exquisite elation which aeronauts know when once they have breathed that rare and sublimated atmosphere—looked down upon the realms below, forgetful of all earthly cares and associations, in the silence of their vast isolation. But they appreciated and enjoyed their unique situation more than any of those who had preceded them, for they added to the pleasures of an aerial voyage the rapture of their own happiness. They spoke in low tones, as if afraid of being overheard by the angels, and of seeing the magic charm dissolved which held them so near to heaven.... Sometimes sudden flashes came to them,—gleams from the aurora borealis; then darkness, deeper and more unfathomable than before, reigned again.

They were floating thus in their starry dream when a quick, shrill noise, like that of a new whistle, sounded in their ears. They listened, leaned far out over the car, and listened again. The noise did not come from the earth. Was it an electrical blast from the aurora borealis? Was it the hiss of some magnetic storm in the upper air? Lightning coming from the depths of space flashed about them and disappeared. They listened breathlessly again. The sound was quite close to them.... It was the gas escaping from the balloon!

Either the valve had partly opened of itself, or they had pressed upon the connecting rope while incautiously moving about in the car; at all events, the gas was escaping.

Spero at once detected the cause of the disquieting noise, and it terrified him, for it was impossible to close the valve again. He examined the barometer, which had begun slowly to rise, while the balloon was beginning to descend. The fall, slow at first, but inevitable, would increase in mathematical proportion. Trying to fathom the abyss below them, he saw the flames of the aurora borealis reflected in the water of an immense lake. The balloon was now descending with great rapidity, and was not more than three thousand metres from the ground. Outwardly calm, but fully conscious of the certain and impending peril, the unfortunate aeronaut threw out one after the other the two sacks left for ballast, then the maps, the instruments, the anchor, and emptied the car; but this lightening of the weight was not enough, and served only to slacken momentarily their accelerated speed. The balloon was now descending, or rather falling, at a tremendous rate, and was but a few hundred metres above the lake. Strong wind-currents blew up and down and whistled in their ears.

The balloon twisted about itself, as if whirled by a waterspout. George Spero felt a sudden and passionate embrace, followed by a long kiss upon his lips. "My master, my god, my all! I love you," she cried; and thrusting aside two of the ropes, she leaped into the empty air. The unballasted balloon shot up again like an arrow. Spero was saved.

Icléa's body made a dull, strange, and frightful sound in the midnight stillness as it fell into the deep waters of the lake. Wild with grief and despair, Spero felt his hair bristling with horror. He opened his eyes wide, but saw nothing. Carried up by the balloon to a height of more than a thousand metres, he clung to the valve-rope, hoping to fall again towards the scene of Icléa's catastrophe; but the rope would not work. He fumbled and hunted, but without avail. In the midst of all he felt under his hand his loved one's veil, where it had caught on one of the ropes,—a thin little veil, still fresh with perfume, and filled with the memories of his lovely companion. He stared at the ropes, thinking he could find the imprint of her little clinging hands, and putting his own where Icléa's had been an instant before, he threw himself out of the car. His foot caught in a rope for a second, but he had strength enough to disengage it, and fell whirling into space.

The crew of a fishing-boat that had witnessed the closing scenes of the drama crowded all sail towards the spot in the lake into which the young girl had fallen, and succeeded in finding and rescuing her. She was not dead; but all the care lavished upon her could not prevent a fever from setting in and making her its prey.

In the morning the fishermen reached a little harbor on the borders of the lake, and carried her to their humble cot; but she did not regain consciousness. "George!" she cried, opening her eyes, "George!" and that was all. The next day she heard the village bell tolling a funeral knell. "George!" she repeated, "George!" His body was found in a terribly mangled condition a short distance from the shore. His fall was more than a thousand metres. It had begun over the lake; but the body, retaining the horizontal impetus given by the moving balloon, had not fallen vertically, it had descended obliquely, as if slipping down a rope following the course of the balloon; and like a mass thrown from the sky, had fallen into a meadow near the shore of the lake, making a deep indentation in the soil, and rebounding more than a metre from the place where it fell. His very bones were crushed into powder, and the brain protruded through the forehead. His grave had hardly been closed before they were obliged to dig another beside it for Icléa, who died murmuring in a feeble voice, "George! George!"

A single stone covers both graves, and the same willow-tree shades their sleep. To this day the dwellers on the shores of beautiful Lake Tyrifiorden remember the melancholy episode, which has become almost legendary; and when the gravestone of the lovers is shown to the tourist, their memory is always associated with a happy, happy dream that has vanished.

VI.
ETERNAL PROGRESS.

DAYS, weeks, months, seasons, years, pass quickly on this planet,—and doubtless also on the others. The Earth has already run its yearly course around the Sun twenty times since destiny so tragically closed the book that my young friends had been reading for less than a year. Their happiness was short-lived; their morning faded away like the dawn.

I had forgotten,[1] or at least lost sight of them, when quite recently, at a hypnotic séance in Nancy, where I had stopped for a few days on my way to the Vosges, I was induced to question a "subject" by whose assistance the experimental savants of the Académie Stanislas had obtained some of those really startling results with which the scientific Press has surprised us for a few years past. I do not remember how, but it happened that my conversation with him turned on the planet Mars. After describing to me a country situated on the shores of a sea known to astronomers under the name of Kepler's Ocean, and a solitary island lying in the bosom of this sea; after telling me about the picturesque landscapes and reddish vegetation which adorned the shores, the wave-washed cliffs, and the sandy beaches where the billows break and die away,—the subject, who was very sensitive, suddenly grew pale, and raised his hand to his head; his eyes closed, his eyebrows contracted; he seemed desirous of grasping some fugitive idea which obstinately eluded him. "*See!*" said Dr. B., standing before him with irresistible command; "see! I wish it."

"You have friends there," he said to me.

"I am not surprised at that," I said, laughing; "I have done enough to deserve them."

"Two friends," he went on, "who are talking about you now, this very minute."

"Ah, ha! Persons who know me?"

"Yes."

"How is that?"

"They have known you here."

"Here?"

"Here,—on the earth!"

"How long ago was it?"

"I do not know."

"Have they lived on Mars long?"

"I do not know."

"Are they young?"

"Yes; they are lovers, who adore each other."

Then the loved image of my lamented friends rose distinctly in my mind; but I had no sooner seen them than the subject exclaimed,—

"Yes! it is they!"

"How do you know?"

"I see,—they are the same souls, same colors."

"What do you mean by the 'same colors'?"

"Yes, the souls are suffused with light."

A few instants afterwards he added, "And yet there is a difference."

Then he was silent, his forehead frowning in his effort to find out. But his face regained all its calmness and serenity as he added,—

"He has become she, the woman; she is now the man,—and they love each other more than ever."

As if he did not quite understand what he had said himself, he seemed to be seeking for some explanation,—made painful efforts, judging from the contraction of the muscles in his face, and fell into a sort of cataleptic fit, from which Dr. B. speedily relieved him; but the lucid interval had fled, not to return.

In ending, I leave this last fact with the reader just as it happened, without comment. Had the subject, according to the hypothesis now admitted by many hypnotists, been under the influence of my own thought when the professor ordered him to answer me? Or, being independent, had he really "freed" himself, and had he *seen* beyond our sphere? I cannot undertake to decide. Perhaps it will appear in the course of this story.

And yet I will acknowledge in all sincerity that the resurrection of my friend and his adored companion on the world of Mars,—a neighboring abode to ours, and so remarkably like this one we inhabit, only older, doubtless more advanced on the road of progress,—may appear to a thinker's eyes the logical and natural continuation of their earthly existence, so quickly broken off.

Doubtless Spero was right in declaring that matter is not what it seems to be, and that appearances are deceitful; that the real is the invisible; that animate force is indestructible; that in the absolute, the infinitely great is identical with the infinitely small; that celestial space is not impassable; and that souls are the seeds of planetary humanities. Who knows but that the philosophy of dynamism may one day reveal the religion of the future to the apostles of astronomy? Does not Urania bear the torch without which every problem is insoluble, without which all Nature would remain to us in impenetrable obscurity? Heaven must explain the earth, the infinite must explain the soul and its immaterial faculties.

The unknown of to-day is the truth of to-morrow.

The following pages will perhaps enable us to form something of an idea of the mysterious link which binds the transitory to the eternal, the visible to the invisible, earth to heaven.

Part Third.
HEAVEN AND EARTH.

I.
TELEPATHY.

THE magnetic séance at Nancy had left a strong impression on my mind. I often thought of my departed friend and his investigations in the unexplored domains of nature and life, of his sincere and original analytical researches on the mysterious problem of immortality; but I could not think of him now without associating him with the idea of a possible reincarnation in the planet Mars.

This idea seemed to me to be bold, rash, purely imaginary if you like, but not absurd. The distance from here to Mars is equal to zero for the transmission of attraction; it is almost insignificant for that of light, since a few minutes are enough for a luminous undulation to travel millions of leagues. I thought of the telegraph, the telephone, and the phonograph; of the influence a hypnotizer's will has on his subject many kilometres distant; and I wondered if some marvellous advance in science might not suddenly throw a celestial bridge between our world and others of its kind in infinity.

For several evenings I could not observe Mars through the telescope without my attention being diverted by many strange fancies. Still, the planet was very beautiful, as it was during all the spring of 1888. Extensive inundations had taken place upon one of its continents, upon Libye, as astronomers had observed before in 1882, and under various circumstances. It was discovered that its meteorology and climatology are not the same as ours, and that the waters which cover about half of the planet's surface are subject to strange displacements and periodical variations, of which terrestrial geography can give no idea. The snow at the boreal pole had greatly diminished,—which proves that the summer on that hemisphere had been quite hot, although less elevated than that of the southern hemisphere. Besides, there had been very few clouds over Mars during the whole series of our observations. But it will be hardly credible that it was not these astronomical facts, however important they might be, and the base of all our conjectures, which most interested me,—it was what the hypnotized man had told me of George and Icléa; the fantastic ideas flitting through my brain prevented me from making a truly scientific observation. I persistently wondered if communication could not exist between two beings very far removed from each other, and even between the living and the dead; and each time I told myself that such a question was of itself unscientific, and showed a positive spirit.

Yet, after all, what is what we call "science"? What is not "scientific" in Nature? Where are the limits of positive study? Is the carcase of a bird really a more scientific thing than its lustrous, colored plumage and its song with its subtle tones? Is the skeleton of a pretty woman more worthy of admiration than her structure of flesh and her living form? Is not the analysis of the mind's emotions "scientific"? Is it not scientific to try to find out whether the mind can see to a distance, and in what manner? And then, how much reason is there in this strange vanity, that we imagine that science has told us all; that we know all there is to know; that our five senses are sufficient to appreciate the nature of the universe? From what we can make out among the forces acting about us,—attraction, heat, light, electricity,—does it follow that there may not be other forces which escape us, because we have no senses to perceive them? It is not this hypothesis which is absurd, it is the simplicity of pedants. We smile at the ideas of the astronomers, philosophers, physicians, and theologians of three centuries ago; three centuries hence, will not our successors laugh in their turn at the affirmations of those who pretend to know everything now?

The physicians to whom fifteen years ago I communicated some magnetic phenomena observed by myself during some experiments, all confidently denied the reality of the facts. I met one of them recently at the Institute. "Oh!" said he, not without a certain wit, "then it was magnetism; now it is hypnotism, and we are studying it."

Moral. Do not deny anything as a foregone conclusion. Let us study and discover; the explanation will come later.

I was in this frame of mind, pacing up and down my library, when my eyes chanced to fall on a pretty copy of Cicero which I had not noticed for some time. I took up a volume of it, opened it mechanically at the first page I came to, and read the following:—

"Two friends arrive at Megara and take separate lodgings; one of them has hardly fallen asleep before he sees his travelling companion beside him, telling him sorrowfully that his host has formed a plan to assassinate him, and begging him to come to his assistance as quickly as possible. The other awakes; but satisfied that he has had a bad dream, loses no time in going to sleep again. His friend appears to him again, and conjures him to hasten, because the murderers are coming to his room. More puzzled, he is astonished at the persistency of this dream, and is on the point of going to his friend; but reason and fatigue triumph, and he goes to bed again. Then his friend comes to him for the third time, pale, bleeding, disfigured. 'Wretch,' said he to him, 'you did not come when I implored you; it is all over now. Avenge me. At sunrise you will meet a cart loaded with manure at the city gate: stop it, and order it to be unloaded; you will find my body hidden in the middle. Give me an honest burial, and pursue my murderers.' So great a tenacity, such minute details, admitted of no further delay or hesitation; the friend rises, hurries to the gate mentioned, finds the wagon there, stops the driver, who is frightened; and soon after the search begins, the body of his friend is found."

This story seemed to come expressly to strengthen my opinion in regard to the unknown quantities in the scientific problem. Doubtless hypotheses are not lacking in reply to the point in question. It may be said that perhaps the circumstance never happened as Cicero tells it, that it has been amplified and exaggerated; that two friends coming to a strange city may fear an accident, that fearing for a friend's life after the fatigue of a journey, in the middle of the quiet night, one might chance to dream that he is the victim of an assassin. As to the episode of the cart, the travellers may have seen one standing in their host's court-yard, and the principle of the association of ideas comes in to bring it into the dream. Yes, these explanatory hypotheses may be made; but they are only hypotheses. To admit that there had really been any communication between the dead man and the living one is also an hypothesis.

Are facts of this kind very rare? It seems not. I remember, among others, a story told me by an old friend of my boyish days, Jean Best, who, with my eminent friend Édouard Charton, founded the *Magasin Pittoresque* in 1883, and died a few years ago. He was a grave, cold, methodical man, a skilful typographical engraver, and a careful business man. Every one who knew him knows how little nervous he was by temperament, and how foreign to his mind were things of the imagination. Well, the following incident happened to him when he was a child between five and six years old.

It was at Toul, his native place. He was lying in his little bed one beautiful evening, but was not asleep, when he saw his mother come into his chamber, cross it, and go into the adjoining drawing-room, whose door was open, and where his father was playing cards with a friend. Now, his mother was ill at Pau at that time. He at once rose from his bed and ran to the drawing-room after his mother, where he looked for her in vain. His father scolded him somewhat impatiently, and sent him back to bed again, assuring him that he had been dreaming.

Then the child, thinking that he must have been dreaming, tried to go to sleep again. But some time afterwards, lying with his eyes open, he distinctly saw his mother pass him for the second time; only now he hurried to her and kissed her, and she at once disappeared. He did not want to go to bed afterwards, and remained in the drawing-room, where his father continued to play cards. His mother died at Pau the same day at that very hour.

I have this circumstance from M. Best himself, who remembered it clearly. How explain it? It may be said that, knowing his mother was ill, the child often thought of her, and had an hallucination which happened to coincide with his mother's death. That is possible. But it may be thought, too, that there was some sympathetic link between the mother and child, and at that solemn moment the mother's soul may really have been in communication with her child. How? one may ask. We know nothing about it. But what we do not know, is to what we know in the proportion of the ocean to a drop of water.

Hallucinations! That is easily said. How many medical works have been written upon this subject! Everybody knows that of Brierre de Boismont. Among the numberless incidents which it relates, let us cite the two following:

"Observation 84. When King James came to England at the time of the London plague, being at Sir Robert Cotton's house in the country with old Camden, he saw, in a dream, his oldest son, who was still a child living in London, with a bleeding cross on his forehead, as if he had been wounded by a sword. Frightened at this apparition, the king began to pray; in the morning he went to Camden's chamber and told him the events of the night; the latter reassured the monarch, telling him he had nothing to torment himself about. That very day the king received a letter from his wife announcing the death of his son, who had died from the plague. When the child appeared to his father, he had the height and proportions of a grown man.

"Observation 87. Mlle. R., a person of excellent judgment, religious, but not a bigot, lived before her marriage at her uncle's house, D., the celebrated physician and a member of the Institute. She was away from her mother, who was attacked by violent illness in the country. One night this young person dreamed that she saw her, pale, disfigured, very near death, and showing deep grief at not having her children with her, one of whom, the curate of a parish in Paris, had emigrated to Spain, the other being in Paris. Soon she heard herself called by her christian name several times; in her dream she saw the persons who were with her mother, thinking she called her little granddaughter, who had the same name, go into the next room for her, when a sign from the sick woman told them it was not she, but her daughter who lived in Paris, whom she wanted to see. Her face showed the grief she felt at the daughter's absence; suddenly her features changed, the paleness of death spread over her face, and she fell back lifeless on her bed.

"The next morning Mlle. R. seemed very sad to D., who begged to know the cause of her grief. She told him all the particulars of the dream which had so greatly distressed her. D., finding her in that frame of mind, pressed her to his heart, acknowledging that the news was only too true, that her mother had just died; he did not enter into further particulars.

"A few months afterwards Mlle. R., profiting by her uncle's absence to put in order his papers, which, like many other savants, he disliked to have touched, found a letter to her uncle relating the circumstances of her mother's death. What was her surprise to read all the particulars of her dream!"

Hallucination! Fortuitous coincidence. Is that a satisfactory explanation? At all events, it is an explanation which explains nothing at all.

A host of ignorant persons, of all ages and trades, clerks, merchants or deputies, sceptics by temperament or habit, simply declare that they do not believe these stories, that there is nothing true about them. That also is not a very good solution of them. Minds accustomed to study cannot content themselves with so trifling a denial. A fact is a fact; we cannot refuse to admit it, even when we cannot in the present state of our knowledge explain it.

Of course medical annals acknowledge that there is really more than one kind of hallucination, and that certain nervous organizations are their dupes. But there is a wide gulf between that and concluding that all psycho-biological phenomena are hallucinations.

The scientific spirit of our century rightly seeks to free all these facts from the deceptive fogs of supernaturalism, inasmuch as nothing is supernatural, and Nature, whose kingdom is infinite, embraces everything. During the last few years a special scientific society has been organized in England for the study of these phenomena,—the Society for Psychical Research. It has at its head some of the most illustrious savants on the other side of the Channel, and has already sent out important publications. These phenomena of sight at a distance are classed under the general title of Telepathy (τὴλε, *far*, πάθος, *sensation*). Rigorous inquiries are made to verify their testimony. Its variety is very great. Let us look through one of these collections[2] together for a moment, and take out a few of the documents which are duly and scientifically established.

In the following recently observed case, the observer was as wide awake as you and I are at this moment. It is about a certain Mr. Robert Bee, who lives at Wigan, England. Here is the curious revelation, written by the observer himself.

"On the 18th of December, 1873, my wife and I went to visit my wife's family at Southport, leaving my parents to all appearance in perfect health. The next afternoon we were strolling on the beach, when I became so depressed that it was impossible for me to interest myself in anything whatever, so that we soon returned to the house.

"All at once my wife showed signs of great uneasiness, and said she was going to her mother's room for a few moments. A minute afterwards I rose from my armchair and went into the drawing-room.

"A lady in walking costume came towards me from an adjacent sleeping-room. I did not notice her features, because her face was turned away from me; still, I spoke to her, and greeted her at once, but I do not remember now what I said.

"At the same time, while she was passing before me, my wife was coming from her mother's chamber, and walked right over the place where I saw the lady, without seeming to notice her. I said at once, in great surprise, 'Who is that lady whom you just met?' 'I met no one,' replied my wife, still more astonished than I was. 'What!' I replied, 'do you mean to tell me that you did not see a lady this very minute who passed by just where you are now? She probably came from your mother's room, and must be now in the vestibule.'

"'It is impossible,' she said; 'there is positively no one in the house at this moment but my mother and ourselves.'

"Sure enough. No strange lady had been there, and the search which we immediately began was without result.

"It was then ten minutes to eight o'clock. The next morning a telegram informed us of my mother's sudden death from heart-disease at exactly that hour. She was then in the street, and dressed precisely like the unknown lady who had passed in front of me."

Such is the observer's story. The inquiries made by the Society for Psychical Research have proved its absolute authenticity and the agreement of the witnesses. It is as positive a fact as a meteorological, astronomical, philosophical, or chemical observation. How can it be explained? Coincidence, you will say. Can a strict scientific criticism be satisfied with this word?

Still another case.

Mr. Frederick Wingfield, living at Belle-Isle en Terre (Côtes-du-Nord), writes that on the 25th of March, 1880, having gone to bed rather late, after reading a part of the evening, he dreamed that his brother, living in the county of Essex, in England, was with him; but instead of answering a question asked him, merely shook his head, rose from his chair, and went away. The impression was so strong that the narrator sprang from his bed half asleep, awaking as his foot touched the floor, and called his brother. Three days later he received news that his brother had been killed by a fall from his horse the same day, March 25th, 1880, in the evening, about half-past eight o'clock, a few hours before the dream just reported.

An inquiry proved that the date of this death was exact, and that the author of this narrative had written his dream in a diary at the very date of the event, and not afterwards.

Still another case.

"Mr. S. and Mr. L., both employed in a Government office, had been intimate friends for eight years. Monday, 19th March, 1883, L. had an attack of indigestion at his office. He went to a druggist's, where he was given some medicine, and was told that his liver was affected. The following Thursday he was no better; Saturday of that same week he was still absent from the office.

"On Saturday evening, March 24th, S. was at home with a headache; he told his wife that he was too warm, which he had not been before for two months; then, after making this remark, he went to bed, and shortly after he saw his friend L. standing before him, dressed as usual. S. noticed even this particular about L.'s clothes, that he had a black band on his hat, and that his coat was unbuttoned; he also had a cane in his hand. L. looked directly at S. and passed on. S. then remembered the sentence in the book of Job, 'A spirit passed before my face; the hair of my flesh stood up.'

"At that moment he felt a chill run all over his body, and felt the hair rise on his head. Then he asked his wife,'What time is it?' She replied,'Ten minutes of nine.' 'I asked you,' he said, 'because L. is dead; I have just seen him.' She tried to persuade him that it was a pure illusion; but he insisted, in the most solemn manner, that nothing could induce him to change his opinion."

This is the story as told by Mr. S. He did not learn of his friend's death until three o'clock on Sunday. L. had died on Saturday evening at about ten minutes of nine.

Agrippa d'Aubigné's historical account of an occurrence at the time of the Cardinal of Lorraine's death is somewhat like this story:—

"The king being at Avignon on December 23d, 1574, Charles, Cardinal of Lorraine, died there. The queen (Catherine de Médicis) had retired to bed earlier than usual, having at her *coucher*, among other persons of note, the king of Navarre, the archbishop of Lyons, the ladies de Retz, de Lignerolles, and de Saunes, two of whom have confirmed this report. As she was hurrying to finish her good-nights, she threw herself back on her bed with a start, put her hands over her face with a loud cry, calling to those about her for help, pointing to the cardinal at the foot of the bed, who, she said, was holding out his hand to her. She cried out several times, 'M. le Cardinal, I have nothing to do with you.' At the same time the king of Navarre sent one of his gentlemen to the cardinal's house, who reported that he had died at that very minute."

In his book on "Posthumous Humanity," published in 1882, Adolphe d'Assier guarantees the authenticity of the following statement, which was reported by a lady of St. Gaudens as having happened to herself:—

"It was before my marriage," she said, "and I slept with my elder sister. One night we had just put out the light and gone to bed. The fire was still burning enough to dimly light the room. Glancing at the fireplace, to my great surprise I saw a priest seated before the fire warming himself. He was a stout man, and had the form and features of an uncle of ours, a priest who lived in the suburbs. I at once spoke to my sister. The latter looked at the fireplace and saw the same apparition. She also recognized our uncle the priest. An indescribable fright took possession of us, and we both cried 'help' as loud as we could. My father, who was sleeping in an adjoining room, aroused by our cries, rose in great haste, and soon came in with a lighted candle in his hand. The phantom had disappeared; we no longer saw any one in the chamber. The next day we learned by letter that our uncle the priest had died the previous evening."

Another fact is reported by the same disciple of Auguste Comte, and sent by him while living in Rio de Janeiro.

It was in 1858. In the French colony of that city, people were still talking about a singular apparition which had taken place there a few years before. An Alsatian family, consisting of a husband, wife, and little girl, still almost a baby, sailed for Rio de Janeiro, where they were to join some compatriots living in that city. The passage was very long, the wife was taken ill, and lacking proper care and nourishment, did not live to reach there. The day she died she fell into a swoon, remained in that state for some time, and when she recovered her senses, said to her husband, who was watching by her side, "I die happy, for now I am easy about the fate of our child. I have just come from Rio de Janeiro. I found our friend Fritz the carpenter's house and street;

he was standing at the door. I showed him our little girl; I feel sure that on your arrival he will recognize and take care of her." That very day, at the same hour, Fritz the Alsatian carpenter, of whom I have just spoken, was standing at the door of the house where he lived in Rio de Janeiro, when he thought he saw one of his compatriots going along the street with a little girl in her arms. She looked at him entreatingly, and seemed to show him the child she was carrying. Her face, notwithstanding its emaciation, reminded him of Latta, the wife of his friend and fellow-countryman Schmidt. Her expression, the singularity of her step, which seemed more like a vision than reality, struck Fritz; and wanting to be sure that he was not the victim of an illusion, he called one of his men who was working in the shop, and who was also an Alsatian from the same locality.

"Look," said he; "do you not see a woman going down the street, holding a child in her arms, and should you not say that it is Latta, our friend Schmidt's wife?"

"I cannot say; I do not see her very distinctly," replied the workman.

Fritz said no more; but the different circumstances of this real or imaginary apparition fixed themselves firmly in his mind, especially the day and hour. Some time after that, Schmidt, his compatriot, arrived, carrying a little girl in his arms. Latta's visit then came into Fritz's mind; and before Schmidt had spoken a word he said to him,—

"I know all, my poor friend: your wife died during the passage. Before she died, she came and showed me her little girl, that I might take care of her. Here is the date and hour."

It was really the day and hour noted by Schmidt on board the boat.

In his work on the Phenomena of Magic, published in 1864, Gougenot des Mousseaux reports the following incident, which he certifies as absolutely authentic:-

Sir Robert Bruce, belonging to the illustrious Scotch family of that name, was mate of a vessel. One day, when sailing near Newfoundland, and while busy with his calculations, he thought he saw the captain seated at his desk, but looked at him attentively, and noticed that it was a stranger, whose cold, fixed look surprised him. He went on deck; the captain noticed his surprise, and asked him what it meant.

"Who is at your desk?" asked Bruce.

"No one."

"Yes, there is some one there. Is it a stranger; and how did he come there?"

"You are either dreaming or joking."

"Not at all. Come down and see for yourself."

They go down to the cabin, but there is no one at the desk. The ship is thoroughly searched, but no stranger is found.

"And yet the man I saw was writing on your slate; the writing must be there still," said he to the captain.

They looked at the slate; it bore these words: "Steer to the northwest."

"This must be your writing, or some one's else on board the ship."

"No; I did not write it."

Every one was told to write the same sentence, and no handwriting resembled that on the slate. "Very well," said the captain; "we will obey these instructions and steer the ship to the northwest; the wind is right, and will admit of our trying the experiment."

Three hours later, the watch perceived an iceberg, and near it a vessel from Quebec, headed for Liverpool, dismantled and covered with people. They were brought off by boats of Bruce's vessel.

As one of the men was climbing up the side of the rescuing vessel, Bruce started, and drew back in great agitation. He recognized the stranger whom he had seen tracing the words on the slate. He reported the strange incident to the captain.

"Will you write 'Steer to the northwest' on this slate?" asked the captain, turning to the new-comer, and offering the side which bore no writing.

The stranger complied with his request, and wrote the desired words.

"Will you acknowledge that to be your ordinary handwriting?" asked the captain, struck with the similarity of the two sentences.

"Of course; how can you doubt it? You saw me write it yourself."

As a reply, the captain turned the slate over, and the stranger was amazed to see his own writing on both sides.

"Did you dream of writing on that slate?" said the Quebec captain to the man who had just been writing.

"No,—at least I have no remembrance of doing so."

"What was that passenger doing at noon?" asks the rescuer of his brother captain.

"The passenger was very tired, and had fallen into a sound sleep, as near as I remember, a little before twelve o'clock. An hour or more later he awoke, and said to me, 'Captain, we shall be saved this very day;' adding, 'I dreamed that I was on board a vessel coming to our relief.' He described the ship and its rigging, and we were very much surprised, when you headed for us, to recognize the exactness of the description."

After a while the passenger said, "It is very strange, but somehow this ship seems quite familiar to me, and yet I was never on it before."

Baron Dupotet, in his article on "Animal Magnetism," reports the following fact, published in 1814 by the celebrated Jung Stiling, who had it from the observer himself, Baron de Sulza, chamberlain to the king of Sweden.

He was going home one night in summer about twelve o'clock, an hour at which it is still light enough in Sweden to read the finest print. "As I reached the family estate," he said, "my father came to the entrance of the park to meet me; he was dressed as usual, and carried a cane which my brother had carved. I greeted him, and we talked together for a long time. We went into the house and up to his bedroom door together. On going into the chamber I saw my father there, undressed, when the apparition instantly faded away. A little while afterwards my father awoke and looked at me inquiringly. 'My dear Edward,' said he, 'God be praised that I see you safe and well! I was greatly distressed about you in my dream. I thought that you had fallen into the water and were in danger of drowning.' Now on that very day," added the baron, "I had been on the river with some friends crab-fishing, and had come very near being dragged down by the current. I told my father that I had seen his double at the park gate, and that we had had a long talk together. He told me that he had often had similar experiences."

In these various stories are seen spontaneous apparitions and appearances which were provoked, so to speak, by the will. Can mental suggestion go so far as that? The authors of the book mentioned above, "Phantasms of the Living," reply affirmatively by seven well-attested examples, of which I will present one to the attention of my readers. Here it is:—

"The Rev. C. Godfrey, living in Eastbourne, in the county of Sussex, having read an account of a premeditated apparition, was so struck thereby that he determined to attempt it himself. On the fifteenth of November, 1886, about eleven o'clock, he concentrated the whole power of his imagination and all the strength of will of which he was master, upon the idea of appearing to a lady, a friend of his, by standing at the foot of her bed. The effort lasted about eight minutes, after which Mr. Godfrey felt very much fatigued, and went to sleep. The next day the lady who had been the subject of the experiment came of her own accord to tell Mr. Godfrey of what she had seen. When asked to make a memorandum, she did so in these words: 'Last night I awoke with a start, feeling that some one had entered my room. I heard, too, a noise which I supposed to be the birds in the ivy outside my window. I then experienced a sort of uneasiness, a vague desire to leave my room and go down to the lower floor. This feeling became so strong that at last I rose, intending to take something to quiet myself. Going up to my room again, I met Mr. Godfrey standing under the great window which lights the staircase. He was dressed as I am accustomed to seeing him, and I noticed that he was looking at something very intently. He stood there motionless while I held up the lamp and looked at him in astonishment. This lasted three or four seconds, after which I continued my way upstairs. He disappeared. I was not frightened, but very much agitated, and could not go to sleep again.' Mr. Godfrey thought, very sensibly, that the experiment which he had tried would have much more importance if it were repeated. A second attempt failed, but the third was successful. Of course the lady upon whom he operated was not apprised of his intention any more than on the first occasion. 'Last night,' she writes, 'Tuesday, December 7th, I retired to bed at half-past ten, and was soon asleep. Suddenly I heard a voice, which said, "Wake up," and I felt a hand touch the left side of my head. [Mr. Godfrey's intention this time was to make her feel his presence by voice and touch.] In an instant I was thoroughly awake. There was a curious noise, like a jews-harp, in the chamber. I felt, too, a cold breath, which seemed to envelop me. My heart began to beat violently, and I distinctly saw a figure leaning over me. The only light in the room came from a lamp outside, making a long stream of light over the toilet-table; this was darkened by the figure. I turned quickly, and it seemed as if the hand fell from my head to the pillow beside me. The figure was bent over me, and I felt it rest against the edge of the bed. I saw the arm on the pillow all the time. I could see the profile of the face but dimly, as if through a haze; it might have been about a minute and a half. The figure had slightly pushed back the curtain, but I noticed this morning that it hung as usual. There is no doubt that the figure was Mr. Godfrey's. I recognized him by the turn of the shoulders and the shape of the face. All the time that he was there, a current of cold air blew through the room as if the two windows had been open.'"

These are *facts*!

In the present condition of our knowledge it would be absolutely foolhardy to seek to explain them; our psychology is not yet far enough advanced. There are a great many things which we are forced to admit, without the power to explain them in any way. To deny what we cannot explain would be pure folly. Could any one explain the world's system a thousand years ago? Even now, can we explain attraction? But science moves, and its progress will be endless.

Do we know the whole extent of the human faculties? The thinker cannot for a moment doubt that there may be forces in Nature still unknown to us,—as, for example, electricity was less than a century ago,—or that there may be other beings in the universe, endowed with other senses and faculties. But is terrestrial man entirely known to us? It does not seem so. There are facts whose reality we are forced to admit, with no power whatever to explain them.

Swedenborg's life offers three of this nature. Let us put aside for a moment planetary and sidereal visions, which appear more subjective than objective. We will remark, by the way, that Swedenborg was a savant of the first order in geology, mineralogy, and crystallography; a member of the Academy of Sciences of Upsala, of Stockholm, and of St. Petersburg; and we will content ourselves with recalling the three following facts.

The 19th of July, 1759, this philosopher landed at Gothenburg on his return from a journey to England, and went to dine with a certain William Costel, where there was quite a large company. At six o' clock in the evening Swedenborg, who had gone out, came back to the drawing-room pale and anxious; he said a great fire had at that moment broken out at Stockholm at the Südermoln, in the street in which he lived, and that the fire was spreading rapidly towards his house. He went out again and returned, lamenting that a friend's house had just been reduced to ashes, and that his own was in the greatest danger. At eight o'clock, after being out again, he said joyfully, "Thanks be to God, the fire has been extinguished at the third house from mine!"

The news of this spread throughout the city, which was all the more excited because the governor gave it attention, and many people were anxious for their property or friends. Two days afterwards the royal messenger brought a report of the fire from Stockholm; there was no disagreement between his account and that which Swedenborg had given. The fire had been extinguished at eight o'clock.

This anecdote was written by the celebrated Emmanuel Kant, who had desired to make an inquiry into the facts, and who adds, "What can be alleged against the authenticity of this occurrence?"

Now, Gothenburg is two hundred kilometres from Stockholm. Swedenborg was then in his seventy-second year.

Here is the second fact:—

In 1761 Madame de Marteville, widow of a minister from Holland to Stockholm, received a demand for the sum of twenty-five thousand Dutch florins (ten thousand dollars), from one of her husband's creditors whom she knew her husband had paid, and a second payment of which would greatly embarrass, almost ruin her. It was impossible to find the receipt. She went to see Swedenborg, and a week later she saw her husband in a dream; he showed her the piece of furniture in which the receipt had been placed, together with a hairpin set with twenty diamonds, which she also believed to be lost. "It was at two o'clock in the morning. Greatly elated, she rose, and found everything at the place indicated. Going back to bed, she slept until nine o'clock. About eleven o'clock, M. de Swedenborg was announced. He told her that he saw M. de Marteville's spirit the night before, and that he informed him that he was going to his widow."

And now for the third fact.

In the month of February, 1772, being in London, Swedenborg sent a note to the Rev. John Wesley (founder of the Wesleyan sect), telling him that he should be very glad to make his acquaintance. The zealous preacher received the note just as he was setting out on a journey, and replied that he should profit by the gracious permission to visit him, on his return, which would be in about six months. Swedenborg answered him "that in that case they would never see each other in this world, as the 29th of the next month was to be the day of his death."

Swedenborg really died on the date mentioned by himself more than a month beforehand.

These are three facts whose authenticity it is impossible to doubt, but which in our present condition of knowledge no one would be able to explain.

We might multiply these *authentic* accounts indefinitely. Facts analogous to those already mentioned of communications from a distance, whether at the moment of death or in the normal condition of life, are not so rare—without, however, being very frequent—but that every one of our readers may have heard such cited, or perhaps have observed them himself in more than one instance. Besides, experiments made in the realms of magnetism show also that under certain ascertained psychological conditions an experimenter can act upon his subject not only at the distance of a few metres, but of several kilometres, and even of more than a hundred kilometres, according to the sensitiveness of the subject, as well as to the intensity of the magnetizer's will. Moreover, space is not what we suppose. The distance from Paris to London is great for a walker, and was even insurmountable before the invention of boats; it is nothing for electricity. The distance from the Earth to the Moon is great for our present modes of locomotion; it is nothing for attraction. In fact, from an absolute point of view, the space which separates us from Sirius is not a greater part of infinity than the distance from Paris to Versailles, or from your left eye to your right.

There is more yet; the separation which seems to us to exist between the Earth and the Moon, or between the Earth and Mars, or even between the Earth and Sirius, is only an illusion due to the insufficiency of our perceptions. The Moon acts constantly upon the Earth, and moves it perpetually. The attraction of Mars for our planet is equally acute, and we in our turn disturb Mars in its course in submitting to the influence of the Moon. We act upon the Sun itself, and make it move as if we touched it. By virtue of attraction, the Moon causes the Earth to turn every month around their common centre of gravity,—a point which travels one thousand seven hundred kilometres below the surface of the globe. The Earth causes the Sun to turn annually around their common centre of gravity, situated four hundred and fifty-six kilometres from the solar centre; all the worlds act upon each other perpetually, so that there is no isolation, no real separation, between them. Instead of being a void separating the worlds from one another, space is rather a connecting link. Now, if attraction thus establishes a real, perpetual, active, and indisputable communication between the Earth and its sisters in immensity, as proved by the precision of astronomical observations, we do not see by what right pretended positivists can declare that no communication can be possible between two beings, more or less distant from each other, either on the Earth or in two different worlds.

Cannot two brains that vibrate in unison at a distance of many kilometres be moved by the same psychic force? Cannot the emotion which starts from a brain reach a brain vibrating at no matter what distance, just as sound crosses a room, making the strings of a piano or violin vibrate?

Do not forget that our brains are composed of molecules which do not touch, and which are in constant vibration. And why speak of brains? Cannot thought, will, psychic force, whatever its nature may be, act on a being to whom it is attached by the sympathetic and indissoluble ties of intellectual relationship? Do not the palpitations of a heart suddenly transmit themselves to the heart which beats in unison with ours? Are we to admit in the cases of apparitions noted above that the mind of the dead has really assumed a corporeal form when near the observer? In the greater part of the cases this hypothesis does not seem necessary. In our dreams we think we see persons who are not before our closed eyes at all. We see them perfectly, as well as in broad daylight; we speak to them, converse with them. Surely it is neither our retina nor our optic nerve which sees them, any more than our ear hears them. Our cerebral cells alone are concerned in it.

Certain apparitions may be objective, exterior, and substantial; others may be subjective,—in that case the being who manifests himself would act from a distance on the being who sees, and this influence on his brain would determine the interior vision which appears exterior, as in dreams, but may be purely subjective and interior. Just as a thought, a memory, may arouse an image in our minds which may be very distinct and very vivid, just so one intelligence acting upon another may make an image appear in him which will for a moment give him the illusion of reality. It is not the retina which is affected by a positive reality, it is the optic thalami of the brain which are excited. In what way? The present state of our physiological and psychological knowledge does not yet teach us that.

Such are the most rational inductions which it seems possible to derive from the phenomena to which we have just been giving our attention,—unexplained, but very old phenomena; for the histories of all peoples, from the highest antiquity, have preserved examples of it which it would be very difficult to deny or efface. But it will be asked, ought we, can we, admit in our age of experimental methods and positive science that a dying or even a dead man can communicate with any one? What is a dead man?

A human being dies every second on the whole terrestrial globe; that is, eighty-six thousand four hundred per day, about thirty-one millions per year, or more than three milliards per century. In ten centuries more than thirty milliards of corpses have been committed to the earth and given back to general circulation under the form of various products,—water, gas, etc. If we keep an account of the diminution of human population as we count up the historic ages, we find that for ten thousand years, *at least two hundred milliards of human bodies have been formed from the earth and from the atmosphere by respiration and nourishment, and have returned to it.* Molecules of oxygen, hydrogen, carbonic acid, and nitrogen, which have constituted these bodies, have enriched the earth and been given back to atmospheric circulation.

Yes, the Earth we inhabit is now formed partly of the milliards of brains which have thought, the milliards of organisms who have lived. We walk over the remains of our ancestors as our descendants will walk over ours. The brows of thinkers; eyes which have looked, smiled, and wept; mouths which have sung of love, rosy lips, and marble bosoms; mothers' flesh and blood; the arms of toilers; the muscles of men, good and bad,—all who have lived, all who have thought, lie in the same earth. It would be difficult now to take a single step on the planet without walking on the remains of the dead; it would be difficult to breathe without inhaling the breath of the dead. The constructive elements of the body draw upon Nature and are returned to Nature, and each one of us bears in himself atoms which have formerly belonged to other bodies.

Ah, well! Do you think that can be all of humanity? Do you think it may not have left something nobler, grander, and more spiritual? Does each of us give the universe, when we breathe our last, nothing but sixty or eighty kilos of flesh and bone which will disintegrate and return to the elements? Does not the soul which animates us endure by the same right as each molecule of oxygen or nitrogen or iron? And all the souls that have lived, do they not still exist?

We have no right to affirm that man is composed solely of material elements, and that the thinking faculty is only one property of the organization. On the contrary, we have the strongest reasons for admitting that the soul is an individual entity, that it is that which governs the molecules to organize the living form of the human body.

What becomes of the invisible and intangible molecules which have composed our body during life? They will belong to new bodies. What becomes of the equally invisible and intangible souls? It may be thought that they also reincarnate themselves in new organisms, each in accordance with its nature, its faculties, and its destiny.

The soul belongs to the psychic world. Doubtless there is on the Earth an innumerable quantity of souls, still heavy and coarse, barely freed from matter, and incapable of conceiving intellectual realities. But there are others who live in study, in contemplation, in the culture of the psychic or spiritual world. Those cannot remain imprisoned on the Earth, and their destiny is to live the Uranian life.

The Uranian soul, even during its terrestrial incarnations, lives in the world of the absolute and divine. It knows that, though dwelling on the Earth, it is really in heaven, and that our planet is a star of heaven.

What is the inner nature of the soul? What are its ways of manifestation? When does its memory become permanent, and maintain with certainty a conscious identity? Under what variety of forms and substances can it live? What extent of space can it overcome? What is the order of intellectual relationship which exists among the different planets of the same system? What is the germinating force which sows the world with seed? When can we put ourselves in communication with the neighboring earths? When shall we penetrate the profound secret of destiny? Mystery and ignorance to-day. *But the unknown of yesterday is the truth of to-morrow.*

It is an historic and scientific fact, and absolutely incontestable, that in all ages, among all peoples, and under the most diverse religious manifestations, the idea of immortality rests invulnerable at the base of human consciousness. Education has given it a thousand forms, but did not invent it. It exists of itself. Every human being coming into the world brings with him, under a form more or less vague, this inner feeling, this desire, this hope.

II.
ITER EXTATICUM CŒLESTE.

THE hours and days that I devoted to the study of these psychological and telepathical questions did not prevent my observing Mars through the telescope, and taking geographical drawings of it, every time that our atmosphere, so often cloudy, would permit. Besides, it may be realized that while in the study of Nature and in science all questions are related to each other, yet that astronomy and psychology are most closely united to each other, since the psychic universe has the material world for its habitat, while astronomy has for its object the study of the regions of eternal life, and we could form no idea of these regions if we did not know them astronomically. In fact, whether we know it or not, we are living now, at this moment, in heavenly regions, and all beings, whatever they may be, are eternally citizens of heaven. It was not without a secret divination of things that antiquity made Urania the Muse of all the sciences.

My mind had been occupied with the planet Mars for a long time, when one day, in a solitary ramble on the edge of a wood, after several hours of July heat, I seated myself at the foot of a clump of oak-trees, and was not long in dropping off to sleep.

The heat was overpowering, the landscape silent, the Seine seemed quiet as a canal at the bottom of the valley. I was strangely surprised on waking up after a few minutes' nap at no longer recognizing the landscape nor the trees, nor the river flowing at the foot of the hill, nor the undulating meadows which stretched far away to the distant horizon. The setting sun was smaller than we are accustomed to see it, the air thrilled with harmonious sounds unknown to Earth, and insects as large as birds were fluttering about on the leafless trees, which were covered with gigantic red flowers. Astonishment made me spring up with so energetic a bound that I found myself on my feet feeling singularly light and buoyant. I had taken but a few steps before it seemed to me that more than half the weight of my body had evaporated during my sleep. This inner sensation struck me even more forcibly than the metamorphosis of Nature spread out before me.

I could hardly believe my eyes or senses. Besides, my eyes were not at all the same. I did not hear in the same way, and I realized at once that my organization had developed several new senses quite different from those of our terrestrial body, especially a magnetic sense, by which one being can communicate with another without the necessity of translating thoughts audibly by words. This sense reminds one of the magnetic needle, which, from a cellar in the Paris Observatory, starts and shivers when an aurora borealis appears in Siberia, or when an electric explosion breaks out in the Sun.

The orb of day had just sunk in a distant lake, and the rosy gleams of twilight were hovering far down the sky, like a last dream of light. Two moons were beginning to shed their rays at different heights: the first, a crescent, hung over the lake in whose bosom the Sun had disappeared; the second, in its first quarter, was much higher, and towards the east. They were very small, and but distantly resembled the immense torch of our earthly nights. It seemed as if they shed their bright but feeble rays regretfully. I looked from one to the other in utter bewilderment. Perhaps the strangest thing in all this strange spectacle was that the western moon, which was about three times as large as its companion in the east, although five times smaller than our terrestrial moon, travelled through the sky with a motion very easy to follow with the eye, and seemed to speed quickly from right to left to join its celestial sister in the west.

A third moon, or rather a brilliant star, could also be seen in the last beams of the setting Sun, which were dying away. Smaller than the smallest of the satellites, it showed no appreciable disk, but its light was dazzling. It looked out from the evening sky as Venus in her most brilliant season beams in our own heavens, when the "shepherd's star" reigns like a queen over balmy evenings in spring, and weaves the fabric of happy dreams.

The more brilliant stars were already lighting up the sky. I recognized Arcturus with its golden rays, Vega so white and pure, the seven stars of the Septentrion, and several of the zodiacal constellations. The evening star, the new vesper, was shining in the constellation of the Fishes. After having studied its position in the heavens for a few moments, and finding out by the constellations where I was myself; after examining the two satellites and reflecting on the lightness of my own body,—I was convinced that I was on the planet Mars, and that the beautiful evening star was—the Earth!

*****

My eyes rested on it with that feeling of mournful love which thrills the fibres of our hearts when our thoughts fly away to a beloved object from whom we are separated by cruel distance; for a long time I looked at that fatherland where so many different feelings meet and jostle each other, and I thought,—

"What a pity it is that the numberless human beings living on that little habitation do not know where they are! That little Earth is most beautiful thus lighted up by the Sun, with its microscopic moon which looks like a speck beside it. Borne through the invisible by the divine laws of attraction, a floating atom in the harmony of the skies, it fills its place and hovers overhead like an angelic island! But its inhabitants are unaware of it! Singular humanity! They find the Earth too wide, so divide themselves up into flocks, and spend their time shooting one another. In that angelic isle there are as many soldiers as there are male inhabitants; they are all in arms against one another, and think it glorious to change the names of countries and the colors of flags, when it would have been so simple a matter to live peacefully. War is the favorite occupation of its nations, and the primordial education of the people. Aside from that, they spend their existence in adoring matter. They do not appreciate intellectual worth, are indifferent to the most wonderful problems of creation, and live an objectless life! What a pity! A citizen of Paris who had never heard the city's name mentioned, nor that of France, would not be more of a stranger than they in their own country. Ah! if they could but see the Earth from here! How delighted they would be to return to it, and how transformed all their ideas would be, both general and individual! Then they would at least know the land they live in; it would be a beginning,—they would study progressively the sublime truths about it, instead of vegetating under a horizonless fog, and after a while they would live the true life, the intellectual life."

*****

"What honor he pays it! One would think he had left friends in that prison yonder!"

I had not spoken, but I distinctly heard this sentence, which seemed like a reply to my inward conversation. Two of the dwellers upon Mars were looking at and had understood me, by virtue of that sixth sense of magnetic perception to which I before alluded. I was somewhat confused, and, I must confess, deeply wounded, by this apostrophe. "After all," I thought, "I love the Earth; it is my country, and I am patriotic." My two neighbors both began to laugh.

"Yes," answered one of them, with unexpected good-nature, "you are patriotic; any one might know that you have just come from the Earth."

And the elder added,—

"Let your compatriots alone. They will never be any more intelligent or less blind than they are now. They have been there eighty thousand years already, and you yourself acknowledge that they are not yet capable of thinking. It is really very absurd of you to look at the Earth with such sorrowful eyes. It is too foolish."

Dear reader, have you not, in your journey through the world, sometimes met men who were puffed up with imperturbable pride, and who thought themselves sincerely and unquestionably above all the rest of the world? When these proud personages find themselves face to face with anything superior, they are instantly hostile to it, they cannot endure it. Very well. In the preceding dithyramb (of which you have had but a very poor translation), I felt myself greatly superior to earthly humanity, since I felt pity for it, and invoked for it better days. But when these two inhabitants of Mars pitied me, and I thought I discovered in them a cold superiority to myself, I was for a moment like these foolish, proud people. My blood gave one bound, and, restraining myself by a remnant of French politeness, I opened my mouth to say,—

"After all, gentlemen, the inhabitants of the Earth are not as stupid as you appear to think, but are worth perhaps more than you."

Unfortunately they did not give me time to begin my sentence, inasmuch as they had understood it all while it was being formed by the vibration of the substance of the brain.

"Permit me to remark at once," said the younger, "that your planet is an absolute failure, in consequence of an occurrence which happened about ten million years ago. It was at the time of the primary period of the earthly genesis. There were plants already, and very fine plants too; the first animals were beginning to appear in the depths of the sea and along the shores,— mollusks that were headless, deaf, mute, and without sex. You know that respiration is all a tree requires for its entire nourishment, and that your most robust oaks, your most gigantic cedars, have never eaten anything, and that that has not prevented their growth. They are nourished solely by respiration. Misfortune, Fatality, had willed that a drop of water thicker than the surrounding medium should pass through one of the mollusks. Perhaps he liked it. That was the first digestive tube, which was to exert so baleful an effect on the entire animal kingdom, and later on mankind itself. The first murderer was the mollusk who ate. Here we do not eat, have never eaten, and never shall eat. Creation is developing itself gradually, peacefully, and nobly, as it began. Organisms are nourished; or, to express it differently, renew their molecules by a simple respiration, like your terrestrial trees, each leaf of which is a little stomach. In your precious country you can live a single day only on condition of killing. With you, the law of life is the law of death. Here, the idea of killing even a bird has never occurred to any one.

"You are all more or less butchers. Your hands are stained with blood, your stomachs are gorged with food. How can you expect to have wholesome, pure, elevated ideas,—I will even say (excuse my frankness) clean ideas,—with such coarse organisms? What souls could live in such bodies? Reflect a moment, and do not soothe yourself any more with blind illusions, too ideal for such a world."

"What!" I cried, interrupting him, "do you deny us the possibility of having clean ideas? Do you take human beings for animals? Have Homer, Plato, Phidias, Seneca, Virgil, Dante, Columbus, Bacon, Galileo, Pascal, Leonardo, Raphael, Mozart, Beethoven, never had lofty aspirations? You think our bodies coarse and repulsive; if you had seen Helen, Phryne, Aspasia, Sappho, Cleopatra, Lucretia Borgia, Agnes Sorel, Diane de Poitiers, Marguerite de Valois, Borghese, Talien, Récamier, Georges, and their charming rivals, you would perhaps think differently. Ah, my dear Martial, let me in my turn regret that you know the Earth only from afar."

"You are mistaken there; I lived in that world for fifty years. That was enough for me, and I assure you I would not return to it again. Everything is a failure there, even—what seems most delightful to you. Do you imagine that in all the earths of heaven the flowers produce the fruits of the same sorts? Would not that be a little cruel? As for me, I like primroses and rosebuds."

"Well, but still," I answered, "notwithstanding all that, there have been great minds on the Earth, and creatures really worthy of admiration. May we not comfort ourselves with the hope that physical and moral beauty will go on perfecting themselves more and more as they have done hitherto, and that intelligence will enlighten itself progressively? We do not spend all our time eating. Men will surely end, in spite of their material labors, by giving up a few hours every day to the development of their understanding. Then probably they will no longer continue to manufacture little gods in their own image; and perhaps also they will abolish their childish boundaries, so that harmony and fraternity may reign."

"No, my friend, for if they wished it, they could do so now; but they are very careful not to. Terrestrial man is a little animal who on the one hand feels no need of thinking, not even having independence of soul, and who on the other likes to fight, and squarely establishes right by might. Such is his good pleasure, and such is his nature. You will never make peaches grow on a thorn-bush. Remember that the most exquisite beauties, to whom you alluded just now, are but coarse monsters compared to the aerial women of Mars, who live on our spring air, the perfume of our flowers, and are so captivating in the very quivering of their wings, in the ideal kiss of a mouth which has never eaten, that if Dante's Beatrice had been of such a nature, the immortal Florentine would never have been able to write two of the parts of his 'Divine Comedy;' he would have begun with Paradise, and could never have left it. Reflect that our youths have as much innate science as Pythagoras, Archimedes, Euclid, Kepler, Newton, Laplace, and Darwin after all their laborious studies; our twelve senses put us in direct communication with the universe; we feel from here Jupiter's attraction as he passes, a hundred million leagues away. We see the rings of Saturn with the naked eye, we detect the coming of a comet, and our body is impregnated with the solar electricity which puts all Nature in vibration. Here there has never been either religious fanaticism or executioners, or martyrs or international divisions or wars, but from the first, humanity, naturally peaceful, and freed from all material needs, has lived independent in body and mind, in a constant intellectual activity, raising itself unhindered to the knowledge of the truth. But come over here."

*****

I walked a few steps on the mountain-top with my new acquaintances, and coming in sight of the other slope, I saw multitudes of different colored lights flitting about in the air. It was the inhabitants, who, when they desire it, become luminous at night. Aerial cars, apparently formed of phosphorescent flowers, were carrying orchestras and choruses; one of them passed us, and we took our places in it, in the midst of a cloud of perfumes. The sensations which I experienced were singularly unlike any which I had ever felt on the Earth, and this first night on Mars passed like a rapid dream; for the dawn found me still in the aerial car conversing with my entertainers, their friends, and their indescribably lovely companions. What a panorama with the rising sun! Flowers, fruits, perfumes, fairy-like palaces rose on the islands with their orange vegetation; the waters stretched themselves out like limpid mirrors, and joyous aerial couples were whirling down to these enchanting shores. There, all material work is done by machines, and directed by a few perfected races of animals whose intelligence is very nearly of the same order as that of mankind on the Earth. The inhabitants live only for and by the mind; their nervous system has reached such a degree of development that each one of these beings, at once very delicate and very strong, seems an electric battery, and their most sensual impressions, felt more by their souls than their bodies, surpass a hundredfold all those that our five terrestrial senses together could ever offer us. A kind of summer palace illuminated by the rays of the rising Sun opened beneath our aerial gondola. My neighbor, whose wings were fluttering with impatience, placed her delicate foot upon a tuft of flowers which rose between two jets of perfume. "Will you return to the Earth?" she asked, holding out her arms to me.

"Never," I cried, springing towards her.

*****

But at that moment I found myself alone near the wood on the slope of the hill, at whose feet the Seine was winding with undulating curves.

"*Never,*" I repeated, trying to grasp the sweet, vanished dream once more. Where had I been? It was beautiful. The Sun had just set, and the planet Mars, then very brilliant, was already shining in the sky. "Ah!" I said, as a fugitive beam reached me, "I have been there!" Drawn by the same attraction, the two neighboring planets are looking at each other through transparent space. May we not catch a first glimpse of the eternal journey from this celestial fraternity? The Earth is no longer alone in the universe. The panoramas of the infinite are beginning to open themselves out. Whether we live here or near by, we are not the citizens of a country or of a world, but are in very truth the *Citizens of Heaven*!

III.
THE PLANET MARS.

HAD I been the plaything of a dream?

Had my spirit really been transported to the planet Mars, or had I been the dupe of a purely imaginary illusion?

The feeling of reality had been so strong, so intense, and the things I had seen agreed so perfectly with the scientific notions which we already possess in regard to the physical nature of the Martial world, that I could not entertain a doubt on the subject, although amazed at that ecstatic trip, and asking myself a thousand questions, each one contradicting the other.

Spero's absence in all that vision puzzled me a little. I still felt so closely attached to his dear memory that it seemed to me as if I should have been able to detect his presence, to fly directly to him, see him, speak to him, hear him. But was not the man hypnotized at Nancy the toy of his own imagination, or of mine, or of the experimenter's? On the other hand, even admitting that my two friends had been reincarnated upon that neighboring planet, I reflected that beings might easily not meet one another in going about the same city, and in a world the chances were infinitely less. And yet surely it was not the doctrine of chances which should be invoked in this case; for such a feeling of attraction as that which had united us ought to increase the probability of our meeting, and throw an element into the scale which should outweigh all the rest.

Talking thus with myself, I went back to my observatory at Juvisy, where I had been preparing some electric batteries for an optical experiment with the tower of Montlhéry. When I had satisfied myself that everything was in readiness, I left the task of making the signals agreed upon, between ten and eleven o'clock, to my assistant, and went to the old tower, where I installed myself an hour later. The night had come. From the top of the old donjon the horizon is perfectly circular, entirely free in all its circumference, which extended on a radius of twenty to twenty-five kilometres all around this central point. A third post of observation, situated in Paris, was in communication with us. The object of the experiment was to find out whether the rays of different colors of the luminous spectrum all travel with the same speed,—300,000 kilometres a second. The result was affirmative.

The experiments were ended at about eleven o'clock, the starry night was marvellous, and the moon was beginning to rise. As soon as I had put the apparatus under cover inside the tower, I went to the upper platform again, to look at the broad landscape lighted by the first rays of the waxing moon. The atmosphere was calm, mild, almost warm.

But my foot was still on the last step when I stopped, terror-stricken, uttering a cry which seemed to die away in my throat. Spero, yes, Spero himself, was there, before me, seated on the parapet! I threw up my arms, and felt as if I were going to faint; but he said in his gentle voice, which I knew so well,—

"Do I frighten you?"

I had not strength enough to reply or to advance, and still I dared to look at my friend, who was smiling at me. His dear face, lighted by the moonlight, was just as I had seen it when he left Paris for Christiania,—young, pleasant, and thoughtful, with a very animated look. I left the stairs, and felt a strong desire to rush to him and embrace him; but I dared not, and stood looking at him.

When I had recovered my senses I cried, "Spero, it is you!"

"I was there during your experiments," he replied, "and it was I who inspired you with the idea of comparing the intense violet with the intense red, for the speed of the luminous waves; only I was invisible, like the ultra-violet rays."

"Can it really be so? Let me look at you and feel you."

I passed my hands over his face and body, through his hair, and had precisely the same impression as if he had been a living being. My reason refused to admit the testimony of my eyes and hands and ears, yet I could not doubt that it was really he. There could not be such a resemblance. And then, too, my doubts would have disappeared at his first words, for he at once added,—

"My body is at this moment sleeping in Mars."

"So," I said, "you still exist, you are living now, and you know at last the answer to the great problem that so distressed you? And Icléa?"

"We will have a long talk," he answered; "I have many things to tell you."

I sat down beside him on the edge of the wide parapet which rises above the old tower, and this is what I heard.

*****

Shortly after the accident at Lake Tyrifiorden he had felt like a man who awakes from a long and heavy sleep. He was alone in midnight darkness on the border of a lake; he knew that he was living, but could neither see nor feel himself. The air did not affect him; he was not only light, but imponderable. Apparently, what remained of him was solely his thinking faculty. His first idea on trying to remember was that he had awakened from his fall by the Norwegian lake; but when the day broke he saw that he was in another world. The two moons revolving rapidly in the sky in opposite directions made him surmise that he was upon our neighbor, the planet Mars, and other evidences soon proved that he was correct.

He lived there for a while in the spirit state, and recognized there the presence of a very beautiful humanity, in which the feminine sex reigns supreme, from an acknowledged superiority over the masculine sex. These organisms are light and delicate, their density of body very slight, their weight slighter still. On the surface of this world material force plays but a secondary part in nature; delicacy of sensation decides everything. There is a large number of animal species, and several human races. In all these species and races the feminine sex is stronger and handsomer (the strength consisting in the superiority of sensation) than the masculine sex, and it is she who rules the world.

His great desire to know the life before him induced him not to remain long as an onlooker in the spirit state, but to come to life again under a corporeal form, and, knowing the organic condition of this planet, in a feminine form.

Among the terrestrial souls floating about in the atmosphere of Mars he had already met Icléa's (for souls feel each other), who had followed him, guided by a constant attraction. She on her part had felt inclined towards a masculine incarnation. Thus they were reunited, in one of the most privileged countries in that world, neighbors and predestined to meet again in life, to share the same emotions, the same thoughts, the same works; thus, although the memory of their earthly life remained veiled and as if effaced by the new transformation, yet a vague feeling of spiritual relationship and an immediate sympathetic attachment had reunited them as soon as they saw each other. Their psychic superiority, the nature of their habitual thoughts, their condition of mind, accustomed to seek ends and causes, had given them both a kind of inward clairvoyance which freed them from the general ignorance of the living. They had fallen in love with each other so suddenly, they had yielded so passively to the magnetic influence of the thunder-clap of their meeting, that they soon formed but a single being, united as at the time of their earthly separation. They remembered that they had met before, and were sure that it must have been on the Earth,—that neighboring planet which shines in the evening so brilliantly in the sky of Mars; and sometimes, in their solitary flights over the little hills peopled with aerial plants, they contemplated the "evening star," trying to re-tie the broken thread of an interrupted tradition.

An unexpected event explained their reminiscences, and proved that they were not mistaken.

The inhabitants of Mars are very superior to those of Earth by their organizations, by the number and delicacy of their senses, and by their intellectual faculties.

The fact that density is very slight on the surface of that world, and that the constituent particles of bodies are less heavy there than here, has permitted the formation of beings of incomparably less weight, more aerial, more delicate, more sensitive. The fact that the atmosphere is nutritive has freed Martial organisms from the coarseness of earthly needs. It is an entirely different state of things. The light there is less bright, that planet being farther from the Sun than we, and the optic nerve is more sensitive. Electric and magnetic influences being very intense, the inhabitants possess senses unknown to terrestrial organizations,—senses which put them into communication with these influences. Everything is evenly balanced in Nature. Beings are everywhere adapted to their surroundings and to the soil from which they spring. Organisms can no more be earthly on Mars than they could be aerial at the bottom of the sea. More than that, the condition of superiority generated by this nature of things is developed of itself by the facility by which all intellectual work is accomplished. Nature seems to obey thought. The architect desirous of erecting a building, the engineer who wants to change the surface of the ground, either to lower or to raise, to cut down mountains or fill up valleys, does not strike against material weight and material difficulties, as he does here. Art, too, has made the most rapid progress from the beginning.

And yet more. Martial humanity, being several hundreds of thousands of years older than terrestrial humanity, went through all the phases of its development before we did; our real scientific progress, even the most transcendent, is but a child's foolish toy, compared to the science of the inhabitants of that planet. In astronomy, especially, they are incomparably more advanced than we, and know the Earth much better than we know their home. They have invented, among other things, a kind of telephotographic apparatus, in which a roll of stuff constantly receives the picture of our world, and is impressed by it unalterably as it unrolls. An immense museum, devoted especially to the planets of the solar system, preserves all these photographic pictures, fixed forever in chronological order.

All the Earth's history is to be found there,—France in the time of Charlemagne, Greece in the days of Alexander, Egypt under Rameses. By the microscope the smallest details can be made out, such as Paris during the French Revolution, Rome under the pontificate of Borgia, Christopher Columbus's Spanish fleet reaching America, the Francs of Clovis taking possession of the Gauls, Julius Cæsar's army stopped in its conquest of England by the tide which washed away his ships, the troops of King David, the founder of standing armies, as well as most historic scenes, recognizable from special characters of their own.

One day, when the two friends were visiting the museum, their reminiscences, which had been thus far very vague, were brightened, like a landscape at night, by a flash of lightning. Suddenly they *recognized* the appearance of Paris during the Exposition of 1867. Their memory became more definite. They each felt, individually, that they had lived there; and under this strong impression they also felt sure that they had lived there together. Their memory gradually grew clearer, not by interrupted gleams, but rather as the light grows stronger from the beginning of dawn.

Then they both remembered, as if by inspiration, that sentence of Scripture: "In my Father's house are many mansions;" and this other, from Jesus to Nicodemus: "Verily, I say unto thee, except a man be born again, he cannot see the kingdom of God.... Ye must be born again."

From that day they never doubted their former earthly existence, but were convinced that they were continuing on the planet Mars the life they had lived before. They belonged to the cycle of the great minds of all ages, who know that human destiny does not end with the present world, but continues in heaven, and who also know that each planet—Mars, the Earth, or any other—is a star of heaven.

The rather singular fact of the change of sex, which seemed to me to be very important, was really without any weight whatever. Spero told me that souls, contrary to our ideas, have no sex, and that their destinies are the same. I also learned that on that planet, so much less material than our own, organisms have no resemblance whatever to terrestrial bodies. Conceptions and births are effected in another way, which reminds one, but under a more spiritual form, of the fecundation and blooming of flowers. Pleasure has no bitterness. Heavy earthly burdens and the anguish of grief are unknown there. Everything there is more aerial, more ethereal, and less material. The Martials might be called winged, sentient, living flowers; but in fact no earthly being can serve as comparison to aid us in imagining their form and manner of existence.

I listened to the translated soul's story almost without interrupting him, for it seemed to me all the time as if he would disappear as he had come. However, remembering my dream, of which I had been reminded by the coincidence of preceding descriptions with what I had seen, I could not keep from telling my celestial friend of that surprising vision, and expressing my surprise at not having seen him on my trip to Mars,—a fact which made me doubt the reality of the journey.

"But," he answered, "I saw you perfectly well, and you both saw and spoke to me, for it was I."

The tones of his voice were so odd at these last words that I suddenly recognized in them the melodious voice of the beautiful Martial girl who had so enchanted me.

"Yes," he answered, "it was I. I was trying to make you know me; but you were so bewildered by a sight which captivated your mind that you did not throw off your terrestrial sensations,—you remained sensual and earthly, you could not rise high enough for pure perception. Yes, it was I who held out my arms to you in the aerial car to take you down to our dwelling, when you suddenly awoke."

"But then," I cried, "if you are that Martial maiden, how can you appear to me in Spero's form, when he no longer exists?"

"I do not act upon your retina or your optic nerve," he replied, "but on your mental being and your brain. I am in communication with you now; I influence directly the cerebral seat of your sensation. My mental being is really formless, like yours and that of all other souls. But when I put myself in direct relation with your thought, as at this moment, you can see me only as you knew me. It is the same during your dreams; that is to say, during more than a quarter of your terrestrial life,—for twenty years out of seventy,—you see, you hear, you speak, you feel, with the same impression, the same clearness, the same certainty as during your normal life; and yet your eyes are closed, your tympanum is insensible, your mouth is mute, your arms are stretched out motionless. It is the same, too, in cases of suggestion, in conditions of hypnotic somnambulism. You see me and hear me, you feel me, too, by your brain, which is under influence; but I am no more in the form which you see than the rainbow exists in the presence of the eyes that look at it."

"Could you also appear to me in your Martial form?"

"No,—at least not unless you were really transported in spirit to that planet. There would then be quite a different mode of communication. In our conversation here, everything is subjective to you. The elements of my Martial form do not exist in the terrestrial atmosphere, and your brain could not imagine them. You can see me to-day only through the medium of your dream; but as soon as you try to analyze its details it will vanish away. You did not see us exactly as we are, because your mind can judge only by your earthly eyes, which are not sensitive to all our radiations, and because you do not possess all our senses."

"I must confess," I answered, "that I cannot understand your Martial beings as having six limbs."

"If these forms were not so graceful, they would have seemed frightful to you; the organisms in each world are most appropriate to its conditions of existence. I acknowledge, on my part, that to the inhabitants of Mars the Apollo Belvedere and the Venus de Médicis are actual monstrosities, on account of their animal heaviness.

"Everything with us is exquisitely light, although our planet is much smaller than yours; yet the beings are larger than here, because the weight is less, and beings can grow taller without being impeded by their weight or imperilling their stability.

"They are larger and lighter, because the constructive materials of that planet are of very little density. What would have happened on the Earth if the weight had not been so great, has happened there. The winged species would have ruled over the world, instead of dwindling away in impossibility of development. On Mars, organic development is effected in the series of winged species. Martial humanity is indeed a race of sextupedal origin; but it is actually bipedal, bimanous, and what might be called *bialic*, since these beings have two wings.

"Their manner of life is totally different from terrestrial life, in the first place because they live in the air and on aerial plants as much as they do on the surface of the ground; and further, because they do not eat, the atmosphere being nutritive. Passions are not the same there. Murder is unknown. Humanity, being without material needs, has never lived there, even in the primitive ages, in the barbarity of rapine and war. The ideas and feelings of the inhabitants of Mars are of an entirely intellectual nature.

"Nevertheless, in dwelling on this planet, analogies at least, if not resemblances, are to be found. Thus, there is a succession of night and day there as on the Earth, which does not differ essentially from what you have, the duration of night and day being 24 hours, 39 minutes, 35 seconds. As there are 668 of these days in a Martial year, we have more time than you for our work, our investigations, and our enjoyments. Our seasons, too, are almost twice as long as yours, but they have the same intensity. The climates are not very different; a country in Mars, on the shores of the equatorial sea, differs less from the climate of France than Lapland differs from Nubia.

"An inhabitant of the Earth would not feel so very foreign. The greatest difference between the two worlds certainly consists in the great superiority of their humanity over yours.

"This superiority is principally due to the great progress realized by astronomical science and to the universal propagation among the inhabitants of that planet of that science, without which one has but false ideas of life, of creation, and of destiny. We are very much favored, as much by the acuteness of our senses as by the purity of our skies. There is much less water on Mars than on the Earth, and fewer clouds. The sky there is almost always fair, especially in the temperate zone."

"But still you often have inundations."

"Yes; and quite recently your telescopes have noticed one along the shores of a sea to which your colleagues have given a name which will always be dear to me, even when far from the Earth. The greater part of our shores are beaches, level plains. We have few mountains, and our seas are not deep. The inhabitants make use of these overflows for irrigating great stretches of country. They have straightened and enlarged the watercourses and made them like canals, and have constructed a network of immense canals all over the continents. The continents themselves are not bristling all over with Alpine or Himalayan upheavals like those of the terrestrial globe, but are *immense plains*, crossed in all directions by canals, which connect all the seas with one another, and by streams made to resemble canals. Formerly there was as much water on Mars, in proportion to the size of the planet, as on the Earth; gradually, from age to age, a part of the rain-water sank into the depths of the soil and did not return to the surface. It combined itself chemically with the rocks, and was withdrawn from atmospheric circulation. Then, too, from age to age, rains, snows, and winds, winter frosts and summer droughts, have disintegrated the mountains, and the watercourses, bringing fragments to the sea-basins, have gradually raised their beds. We have no more large oceans or deep seas,—nothing but inland waters; many straits, gulfs, and seas analogous to the Channel, the Red Sea, the Adriatic, the Baltic, and the Caspian; pleasant shores, quiet harbors, large lakes and streams, aerial rather than aquatic fleets, an almost always clear sky, especially in the morning. There are no mornings on Earth so luminous as ours.

"The meteorological system differs materially from that of the Earth, because, the atmosphere being more rarified, the waters which move over the surface evaporate more easily, and then because in condensing again, instead of forming clouds that last, they pass almost without transition from the gaseous to the liquid state. There are few clouds and few fogs.

"Astronomy is cultivated there on account of the clearness of the heavens. We have two satellites, whose courses would appear strange to earthly astronomers, for while one of them gives us months of a hundred and thirty hours, or five Martial days, plus eight hours, the other, by a combination of its motion with the daily rotation of the planet, rises in the occident and sets in the orient, crossing the sky from west to east in five hours and a half, and passing from one phase to the other in less than three hours. That spectacle is unique in the whole solar system, and has done much to attract the attention of the inhabitants to the study of the sky. Besides that, we have eclipses of the moon almost every day, but never total eclipses of the Sun, because our satellites are too small.

"The Earth looks to us as Venus looks to you. To us it is the morning and evening star; and in old times, before the invention of optical instruments, which have taught us that it is a planet, dwelt upon like ours, but by an inferior race, our ancestors worshipped it as a tutelary divinity. All worlds have a mythology during their centuries of infancy, and this mythology has for its origin, its foundation, and its object the appearance of the celestial bodies.

"Sometimes the Earth, accompanied by the Moon, passes between us and the Sun, and projects itself upon its disk like a little black spot, attended by a still smaller one. Every one there follows these celestial phenomena with curiosity. Our newspapers think more of science than of theatres, literary fancies, or political quarrels.

"The Sun looks smaller to us, and we receive a little less light and heat from it; our more sensitive eyes see better than yours. The temperature is a little higher."

"How can that be?" said I. "You are farther from the Sun, yet are warmer than we?"

"Chamounix is a little farther from noonday sun than Mont Blanc," he answered. "The distance from the Sun does not alone regulate the temperature, you must also take into account the constitution of the atmosphere. Our polar ice melts under our summer sun more entirely than yours."

"What lands in Mars are most populous?"

"There is very little, except the polar regions (where, from the Earth, you see the snow and ice melt every spring), which is uninhabited. The population of the temperate regions is very dense, but in the equatorial lands it is more so; the population there is as dense as in China,—and especially the sea-coasts, notwithstanding the inundations. A large number of cities are built almost on the water, suspended in the air in some way above the overflows, which are calculated and expected beforehand."

"Are your arts and your industries like ours? Have you railways, steamships, the telegraph, and the telephone?"

"It is all quite different. We have never had either steam or railways, because we have always known of electricity, and aerial navigation is natural to us. Our fleets are moved by electricity, and are more aerial than aquatic. We live principally in the air, and have no homes of stone, iron, or wood. We do not experience the rigors of winter, because no one stays exposed to them. Those who do not dwell in the equatorial countries emigrate every autumn, just as your birds do. It would be very difficult for you to form an exact idea of our manner of life."

"Are there many human beings on Mars who have already lived on the Earth?"

"No; among the inhabitants of your planet the greater part are either ignorant, sceptical, or indifferent, and are unprepared for the spiritual life. They are attached to the Earth, and their attachment lasts for a long time. Many souls sleep completely. Those which act, live, and aspire to know the truth, are the only ones called to conscious immortality, the only ones whom the spirit-world interests, and who are capable of understanding it. These souls can leave the Earth and live in other lands. Many come and live for a while on Mars (the first stage of an ultra-terrestrial journey, going from the Sun), or on Venus, the first abode going the other way; but Venus is a world analogous to the Earth, and still less favored, on account of its too rapid seasons, which oblige its inhabitants to suffer the most sudden changes of temperature. Certain spirits wing their way at once to the starry regions. As you know, space has no existence. To sum up, justice reigns in the moral world as equilibrium does in the physical world; and the destiny of souls is but the perpetual result of their capabilities, their aspirations, and consequently of *their works*. The Uranian way is open to all; but the soul becomes truly Uranian only when it has entirely shaken off the weight of material life. The day will come, even on your planet, when there will be no other belief, no other religion, than the knowledge of the universe and the certainty of immortality in its infinite regions, in its eternal domain."

"What a strange thing," said I, "that no one on the Earth should know these sublime truths! No one looks at the sky; we live as though our little isle alone existed in the universe."

"Terrestrial humanity is young," answered Spero. "You must not despair. It is a child, and still in primitive ignorance. It is amused at trifles, and obeys masters of its own giving. You like to divide yourselves into nations, to trick yourselves out in national costumes, and to exterminate each other to music! Then you raise statues to those who have led you to butchery. You ruin yourselves, you commit suicide, and yet you cannot live without wresting your daily bread from the Earth. That is a sad condition of things, but one which fully satisfies the greater part of the dwellers on your planet. If some of them, with higher aspirations, think occasionally of problems of the higher order, of the nature of the soul or the existence of God, the result has been no better, because they have put their souls outside of Nature, and have invented strange, horrible gods, who never existed except in their perverted imaginations, and in whose name they have committed all kinds of outrages against the human conscience, have blessed all crimes, and bound weak minds in a slavery from which it will be difficult for them to escape. The lowest animal on Mars is better, finer, gentler, more intelligent, and greater than the god of the armies of David, Constantine, Charlemagne, and all your crowned assassins. There is therefore nothing surprising in the coarseness and stupidity of terrestrial humanity. But the law of progress governs the world. You are more advanced than at the period of your ancestors of the stone age, whose wretched existence was spent in fighting night and day with ferocious beasts. In a few thousands of years you will be more advanced than you are now. Then Urania will reign in your hearts."

"It would require a brutal material fact to teach and convince human beings. If, for instance, we could some day enter into communication with the neighboring world which you inhabit, not into physical communication with one isolated person of it, as I am now doing, but with the planet itself, by hundreds and thousands of witnesses, that would be a gigantic stride towards progress."

"You could do it now if you chose, for we Martials are all prepared for it, and have even tried it many times. But you have never replied to us. Solar reflections, showing geometrical figures on our vast plains, prove to you that we exist. You could reply to us by like figures also displayed on your plains, either during the day by the sun, or during the night by the electric light. But you never even think of it; and if some one should propose to try it, your courts would interpose to prevent it, for the very idea is immeasurably too high for the general approval of the denizens of your planet. What do your scientific assemblies work for? The preservation of the past. To what do your political assemblies direct their attention? Increasing the taxes. In the land of the blind, one-eyed men are kings.

"But you must not utterly despair. Progress bears you on in spite of yourselves. One of these days, too, you will realize that you are citizens of the sky; then you will live in the light, in knowledge, in the mind's true world."

While the inhabitant of Mars was teaching me the principal characteristics of his new country, the terrestrial globe had turned towards the east, the horizon had sunk lower, and the Moon had gradually risen in the sky, which she was illuminating with her radiance.

Suddenly chancing to lower my eyes to where Spero sat, I could not repress a start of surprise. The moonlight was streaming over him as it did over me, and yet, although my body cast a shadow on the parapet, his figure was shadowless. I arose abruptly to assure myself of this fact. I turned about at once and stretched out my hand to touch his shoulder, watching the shadow of my gesture on the parapet. But my visitor had instantly disappeared. I was absolutely alone on the silent tower. My very dark shadow was thrown out sharply on the parapet. The Moon was brilliant, the village was sleeping at my feet. The air was mild and very still. And yet I thought I heard footsteps. I listened, and indeed did hear rather heavy footsteps coming towards me. Some one was evidently climbing the tower-stairs.

"Monsieur has not gone down yet?" said the custodian, coming up to the top. "I was waiting to lock the doors, and thought the experiments must be over."

IV.
THE FIXED POINT IN THE UNIVERSE.

THE memory of Urania and the celestial journey on which she had borne me away, the truths she had made me realize, Spero's history, his trials in his pursuit of the absolute, his apparition, his story of another world, still haunted me, and kept the same problems (partly solved, partly veiled in the uncertainty of our knowledge) incessantly before my mind. I felt that I had gradually risen to a perception of the truth, and that the visible universe was really but an appearance, which we must pass through in order to reach reality.

The testimony of our senses is but an illusion. The Earth is not what it seems to be. Nature is not what we think. In the physical universe itself, where is the fixed point upon which material creation is in equilibrium?

The natural and direct impression given by the observation of Nature is that we inhabit a solid, stable Earth, fixed in the centre of the universe. It took long centuries of study and a great deal of boldness to free ourselves from that natural conviction, and to realize that the world we are on is isolated in space, without any support whatever, in rapid motion on itself and around the Sun. But to the ages before scientific analysis, to primitive peoples, and even to-day to three quarters of the human race, our feet are resting on a solid Earth which is fixed at the base of the universe, and whose foundations are supposed to extend into the depths of the infinite.

And yet from the time when it was first realized that it is the same Sun which rises and sets every day; that it is the same Moon, the same stars, the same constellations which revolve about us, those very facts forced one to admit with absolute certainty that there must be empty space underneath the Earth, to let the stars of the firmament pass from their setting to their rising. This first recognition was a turning-point. The admission of the Earth's isolation in space was astronomy's first triumph. It was the first step, and indeed the most difficult one. Think of it! To give up the foundations of the Earth! Such an idea would never have sprung from any brain without the study of the stars, or indeed without the transparency of the atmosphere. Under a perpetually cloudy sky, human thoughts would have remained fixed on terrestrial ground like the oyster to the rock.

The Earth once isolated in space, the first step was taken. Before this revolution, whose philosophical bearing equals its scientific value, all manner of shapes had been imagined for our sublunary dwelling-place. In the first place, the Earth was thought to be an island emerging from a boundless ocean, the island having infinite roots. Then the Earth, with its seas, was supposed to be a flat, circular disk, all around which rested the vault of the firmament. Later, cubic, cylindrical, polyhedric forms, etc., were imagined. But still the progress of navigation tended to reveal its spherical nature, and when its isolation, with its incontestable proofs, was recognized, this sphericity was admitted as a natural corollary of that isolation and of the circular motion of the celestial spheres around the supposed central globe.

The terrestrial globe being from that time recognized as isolated, to move it was no longer difficult. Formerly, when the sky was looked upon as a dome crowning the massive and unlimited Earth, the very idea of supposing it to be in motion would have been not only absurd but untenable. But from the time that we could see it in our minds, placed like a globe in the centre of celestial motion, the idea of imagining that perhaps this globe could revolve on itself, so as to avoid obliging the whole sky and the immense universe to perform this daily task, might come naturally into a thinker's mind; and indeed we see the hypothesis of the daily rotation of the terrestrial sphere coming to light in ancient civilizations, among the Greeks, the Egyptians, the Indians, etc. It is sufficient to read a few chapters of Ptolemy, Plutarch, or Surya-Siddhanta for an account of these conjectures. But this new hypothesis, although it had been prepared for by the first one, was none the less bold, and contrary to the feelings inspired by the direct contemplation of Nature. Thoughtful mankind was obliged to wait until the sixteenth century, or, to speak more correctly, until the seventeenth century, to learn our planet's true position in the universe, and to *know* by supported proofs that it has a double movement,—daily about itself, and yearly about the Sun. From that time only, from the time of Copernicus, Galileo, Kepler, and Newton, has real astronomy existed.

And yet again, that was but a beginning, for the great remodeller of the world's system, Copernicus himself, had no suspicion of the Earth's other motions, or of the distances of the stars. It is only in our own century that the first measurements of the distances of the stars could be made, and it is only in our day that sidereal discoveries have afforded us the necessary data by which we might endeavor to account for the forces which maintain the equilibrium of creation.

The ancient idea of endless roots attributed to the Earth, evidently left much to be desired to minds anxious to go to the bottom of things. It is absolutely impossible for us to conceive of a material pillar, as thick and as wide as you like (of the diameter of the Earth, for example), sinking down into the infinite; just as one cannot admit the real existence of a stick which should have but one end. No matter how far our mind goes down towards the base of such a material pillar, there is a point where it can see the end of it. The difficulty had been obviated by materializing the celestial sphere and putting the Earth inside it, occupying all its lower portion. But in the first place it became difficult to adjust the motion of the stars, and on the other hand this material universe itself, enclosed in an immense crystal globe, was held up by nothing, since the infinite must extend all around, beneath it, as well as above. Investigating minds were at first obliged to free themselves from the vulgar idea of weight.

Isolated in space like a child's balloon floating in the air, and more absolutely too, for the balloon is carried by aerial waves, while worlds gravitate in the void, the Earth is a toy for the invisible cosmic forces which it obeys,—a real soap-bubble, sensitive to the faintest breath. Besides, we can easily judge of it by looking at the same time at the whole of the *eleven* principal motions of the Earth, by which it is moved. Perhaps they will help us to find that "fixed point" which our philosophical ambition asks for.

Thrown around the Sun at a distance of 37,000,000 leagues, and making at this distance its annual revolution around the luminous star, it consequently moves at the rate of 643,000 leagues per day; that is, 26,800 leagues an hour, or 29,450 metres per second. This speed is eleven hundred times more rapid than an express train going at the rate of a hundred kilometres an hour. It is a ball, going with a rapidity seventy-five times greater than that of a bomb, always hurrying on, but never reaching its goal. In 365 days, 6 hours, 9 minutes, and 10 seconds, the terrestrial projectile has returned to the same point of its orbit relative to the Sun, and continues its flight. The Sun, on its part, is moving in space, following a line oblique to the plane of the Earth's annual motion,—a line drawn towards the constellation of Hercules. The result is, that instead of describing an exact circle, the Earth describes a spiral, and has never passed over the same road twice in its existence. To its motion of annual revolution around the Sun there is added perpetually, as a second motion, that of the Sun itself, which draws it, with all the solar system, into an oblique descent towards the constellation of Hercules.

During all this time our little globe pirouettes around itself every twenty-four hours, and gives us the daily succession of days and nights,—diurnal rotation: third motion.

It does not turn upright upon itself, like a top, which would be vertical on a table, but is inclined, as everybody knows, by 23° 27'. This inclination, too, is not always the same; it varies from year to year, from age to age, oscillating slowly by secular periods. That is a fourth kind of motion.

The orbit in which our planet yearly travels around the Sun is not circular, but elliptical. This ellipse itself also varies from year to year, and from century to century; sometimes it approaches the circumference of a circle, sometimes it lengthens out to a great eccentricity. It is like an elastic ring, which can be bent more or less out of shape. Fifth complication in the Earth's motion.

This ellipse itself is not fixed in space, but revolves in its own plane in a period of 21,000 years. The perihelion, which at the beginning of our era was at 65 degrees of longitude, starting from the vernal equinox, is now at 101 degrees. This secular displacement of the line of the apsides brings a sixth complication to the motion of our abiding-place.

Here is a seventh. We said just now that our globe's axis of rotation is inclined, and everybody knows that the imaginary prolongation of this axis points towards the polar star. This axis itself is not fixed. It revolves in 25,765 years, keeping its inclination of 22 to 24 degrees, so that its prolongation describes a circle of 44 to 48 degrees in diameter—according to the epoch—on the celestial sphere around the pole of the ecliptic. It is in consequence of this displacement of the pole that Vega, in twelve thousand years, will again become the polar star, as she was fourteen thousand years ago. Seventh kind of movement.

An eighth motion, due to the action of the Moon on the equatorial swelling of the Earth, that of nutation, causes the pole of the equator to describe a small ellipse in eighteen years and eight months.

A ninth, due also to the attraction of our satellite, incessantly changes the position of the globe's centre of gravity and the Earth's place in space. When the Moon is in front of us, she accelerates the speed of the globe; when she is behind, she retards us, on the contrary, like a check-rein,—a monthly complication which is added to all the others.

When the Earth passes between the Sun and Jupiter, the attraction of the latter, in spite of its distance of 155,000,000 leagues, makes it deviate by 2 m. 10 sec. from its absolute orbit. The attraction of Venus makes it deviate 1 m. 25 sec. the other way. Saturn and Mars also act upon it, but more feebly. These are exterior disturbances, which make up a tenth kind of correction to add to the motion of our celestial barque.

The whole of the planets weigh about one seven hundredth part of the weight of the Sun; the centre of gravity around which the Earth annually turns is not in the very centre of the Sun, but far from the centre, and often even outside of the solar globe. Now, absolutely speaking, the Earth does not turn around the Sun; but the two heavenly bodies, Sun and Earth, turn about their common centre of gravity. Thus the centre of our planet's annual motion is constantly changing place, and we may add this eleventh complication to the others. We might even add many others to these; but the preceding ones are enough to make the degree of lightness and delicacy of our floating island appreciated, subject, as we have seen, to all the fluctuations of celestial influences. Mathematical analysis goes very far beyond this summary statement. It has found that the Moon alone, which seems to turn so peacefully about us, has more than sixty distinct motions.

The expression is therefore not exaggerated: our planet is but the plaything of the cosmic forces which accompany it in the meadows of the sky, and it is the same with everything existing in the universe. Matter is meekly obedient to force.

Where, then, is the fixed point which we desire for our support?

Our planet, then, formerly supposed to be at the base of the universe, is in fact kept up at a distance by the Sun, which makes the Earth gravitate about it with a speed corresponding to that distance. This speed, caused by the solar mass itself, keeps our planet at the same mean distance from the central star. A lesser speed would make the weight predominate, and would lead to the Earth's falling into the Sun; a greater speed, on the contrary, would progressively and infinitely send our planet away from its life-giving focus. But at the speed resulting from gravitation, our wandering home remains suspended in permanent stability, just as the Moon is upheld in space by the force of the Earth's gravity, which makes it circulate about the Earth with the speed requisite to maintain it constantly at the same mean distance. The Earth and the Moon thus form a planetary couple in space which sustain each other in perpetual equilibrium under the supreme domination of solar attraction. If the Earth existed alone in the universe, it would be forever motionless in the void, wherever it had been placed, with no power to descend or rise or change its position in any way whatsoever; these very expressions—to rise, descend, left or right—having no absolute sense whatever. If this same Earth, while existing alone, had received any impetus whatever, had been thrown with any speed in any direction, it would have whirled away forever in a straight line in that direction, never being able to stop or to slacken its pace or change its motion. It would have been the same thing if the Moon had existed alone with it; they would both have turned about their common centre of gravity, fulfilling their destiny in the same place in space, flying together, following the direction in which they had been thrown. The Sun existing and being the centre of its system, the Earth, all the planets and their satellites, are dependent upon it, and to it their destiny is irrevocably bound.

Is the fixed point that we are seeking, the solid base which we seem to need to insure the stability of the universe, to be found in that colossal and heavy globe, the Sun?

Assuredly not, since the Sun itself is not in repose, for it is bearing us and all its system away towards the constellation of Hercules.

Does our Sun gravitate around an immense sun whose attraction extends to it and controls its destinies as it controls that of the planets? Do investigations in sidereal astronomy lead us to believe that a star of such magnitude can exist in a direction situated at right angles with our course towards Hercules? No; our Sun is influenced by sidereal attraction, but no one star appears to overpower all the others and reign sovereign over our central star.

Although it may be perfectly admissible, or rather certain, that the sun nearest to ours, the star Alpha Centauri, and our own Sun feel their mutual attraction; although this star may be situated at about 90 degrees from our tangent towards Hercules, and, more than that, in the plane of the principal stars, passing by Perseus, Capella, Vega, Aldebaran, and the Southern Cross; and although the proper motion of this neighboring sun may be turned sensibly in the opposite direction from ours,—yet we could not consider these two systems as forming one couple analogous to that of the double stars; in the first place, because all the known double-star systems are composed of stars much nearer to each other, and then because in the immensity of the orbit described, according to this hypothesis, the attraction of the neighboring stars could not be considered as remaining without influence; and lastly, because the actual rates of speed with which these two suns are moved are much less great than those which would result from their mutual attraction.

The little constellation of Perseus, especially, might very well exert a more powerful action than that of the Pleiades, or than any other group of stars, and be the fixed point, the centre of gravity, of the motions of our Sun, of Alpha Centauri, and the neighboring stars, inasmuch as the cluster of Perseus is not only at right angles with the tangent of our movement towards Hercules, but also in the great circle of the principal stars and precisely at the intersection of this circle with the Milky Way. But here another factor comes in, of more importance than all the preceding ones,—this Milky Way, with its eighteen millions of suns, of which it would assuredly be audacious to seek the centre of gravity.

But what is the whole entire Milky Way, after all, compared with the milliards of stars which our mind contemplates in the bosom of the sidereal universe? Is not this Milky Way itself moving like an archipelago of floating islands? Is not every resolvable nebula, each cluster of stars, a Milky Way in motion under the action of the gravitation of other universes, which call to it and appeal to it through the infinite night?

*****

Our thoughts are transported from star to star, from system to system, from region to region, in the presence of unfathomable grandeurs, in sight of celestial motions whose speed we are but just beginning properly to value, but which already surpasses all conception. The proper annual motion of the sun Alpha Centauri exceeds 188 millions of leagues per year. The proper motion of the 61st of Cygnus (second sun in the order of distances) is equivalent to 370 millions of leagues per year, or about one million of leagues per day. The star Alpha Cygni comes to us in a direct line at a speed of 500 millions of leagues per year. The proper motion of the star 1830 of Groombridge's Catalogue rises to 2,590 millions of leagues per year, which represents seven millions of leagues per day, 115,000 kilometres per hour, or 320,000 metres per second! These are minimum estimates, inasmuch as we certainly do not see perpendicularly, but obliquely, the stellar displacements thus measured.

What projectiles! They are suns thousands and millions of times heavier than the Earth, launched through the unfathomable void with giddy rates of speed, revolving in immensity under the influence of the gravitation of all the stars of the universe. And these millions and thousand millions of suns, planets, clusters of stars, nebulæ, worlds in their infancy, worlds near their end, rush with equal velocity towards goals of which they are ignorant, with an energy and intensity of action before which gunpowder and dynamite are like the breath of sleeping babes.

And thus everything hurries on through all eternity perhaps, without being able ever to reach the unexisting limits of infinity.... Motion, activity, light, life everywhere. Happily so, without doubt. If all these innumerable suns, planets, earths, moons, comets, were fixed and immovable, petrified kings in their eternal tombs, how much more formidable, but also more mournful, would be the aspect of such a universe! Can you imagine the whole creation stopped, benumbed, mummified? Is not such an idea unbearable? Is there not something funereal about it?

What causes these motions? What maintains them? What regulates them? Universal gravitation, invisible force, which the visible universe (what we call matter) obeys. A body attracted from infinity by the Earth would attain a velocity of 11,300 metres per second; just as a body thrown from the Earth with that speed would never fall again. A body attracted by the Sun from the infinite would attain a speed of 608,000 metres; and a body thrown by the Sun with that swiftness would never return to its point of departure. Clusters of stars may give us velocities much more remarkable still, but which are explained by the theory of gravitation. A glance at a map of the proper motions of the stars is enough to make one understand the variety and grandeur of these motions.

*****

Thus the stars, the suns, the planets, the worlds, the shooting-stars, the meteoric stones, in short all the bodies which constitute this vast universe, rest, not on solid bases, as the childish and primitive conception of our fathers seemed to require, but *upon invisible and immaterial forces* which govern their motions. These milliards of celestial bodies have their respective movements for the purpose of stability, and mutually lean upon each other across the void which separates them. The mind which could eliminate time and space would see the Earth, the planets, the Sun, the stars, rain down from a limitless sky in all imaginable directions, like the drops carried away by the whirlwinds of a gigantic tempest, and drawn, not by a common basis, but by the attraction of each and all; each one of these cosmic drops, each one of these worlds, each one of these suns, is whirled away at a speed so rapid that the flight of cannon-balls is but rest in comparison: it is not one hundred, nor five hundred, nor a thousand metres per second,—it is ten thousand, twenty, fifty, a hundred, and even two or three hundred thousand metres *per second!*

How is it that there are no meetings in the midst of all this motion? Perhaps there may be some,—the "temporary stars," which appear to rise again from their ashes, would seem to indicate it. But as a matter of fact, it would be difficult for meetings to occur, because space is immense, relatively to the celestial bodies, and because the motion by which each body is animated entirely prevents it from submitting passively to the attraction of another body and falling upon it; it keeps its own motion, which cannot be destroyed, and glides around the focus which attracts it, as a butterfly would obey the attraction of a flame without burning itself in it. Besides, absolutely speaking, these motions are not "rapid."

Indeed, everything runs, flies, falls, rolls, rushes through the void, but at such respective distances that it all appears to be at rest. If we wanted to place in a frame, the size of Paris, the stars whose distances have been measured up to the present time, the nearest star would be placed at two kilometres from the Sun, from which the Earth would be distant one centimetre, Jupiter at five centimetres, and Neptune at thirty centimetres. The 61st of Cygnus would be at four kilometres, Sirius at ten kilometres, the polar star at twenty-seven kilometres, etc.; and the immense majority of the stars would remain outside the department of the Seine. Well, to give to all these projectiles their relative motions, the Earth would take a year to run through its orbit of a centimetre radius, Jupiter twelve years to run through his of five centimetres, and Neptune one hundred and sixty-five years. The proper motions of the Sun and stars would be of the same nature; that is to say, all would appear to be at rest, even under the microscope. Urania reigns with calmness and serenity in the immensity of the universe.

So the constitution of the sidereal universe is just like that of the bodies which we call material. All bodies, organic or inorganic, man, animal, plant, stone, iron, bronze, are composed of molecules which are in perpetual motion, and which do not touch one another. Each one of these atoms is infinitely small, and invisible not only to the eye, not only to the microscope, but even to thought; since it is possible that these atoms may be centres of force. It has been calculated that in the head of a pin there are not less than eight sextillions of atoms,—that is, eight thousand milliards of milliards,—and that in one centimetre of cubic air there are not less than a sextillion of molecules. All these atoms, all these molecules, are in motion under the influence of the forces which govern them; and as compared with their dimensions, great distances separate them. We may even believe that there is in principle but one kind of atoms, and that it is the number of primitive atoms, essentially simple and homogeneous, their modes of arrangement, and their motions, which constitute the diversity of molecules; a molecule of gold, of iron, would not differ from a molecule of sulphur, of oxygen, of hydrogen, etc., except in the number, the disposition, and the motion of the primitive atoms which compose it: each molecule would be a system, a microcosm.

But whatever may be the idea that one conceives of the inner constitution of bodies, the truth is now recognized and indisputable that the fixed point for which our imagination has been seeking, exists nowhere. Archimedes can vainly call for a point of support, that he may lift the world. *Worlds, like atoms, rest on the invisible*, on immaterial force; everything moves, urged on by attraction, and as if in search of that fixed point which flies as it is pursued, and which does not exist, since in the infinite the centre is everywhere and nowhere. So-called positive minds, which assert with so much assurance that "Matter reigns alone, with its properties," and who smile disdainfully at the researches of thinkers, should first tell us what they mean by that famous word "matter." If they did not stop at the surface of things, if they even suspected that appearances hid intangible realities, they would doubtless be a little more modest.

To us, who seek the truth with no jealousy of system, it seems that the essence of matter remains as mysterious as the essence of force; the visible universe not being in the least what it appears to be to our senses. In fact, that visible universe is composed of invisible atoms; it rests upon the void, and the forces which govern it are in themselves immaterial and invisible. It would be less bold to think that matter does not exist, that all is dynamism, than to pretend to affirm the existence of an exclusively material universe. As to the material support of the world, it disappeared—a somewhat interesting observation—precisely with the conquest of Mechanics, which proclaim the triumph of the invisible. The fixed point vanishes in the universal balance of powers, in the ideal harmony of ether vibrations; the more one seeks it, the less one finds it; and the last effort of our thought has for a last support, for supreme reality, the Infinite.

A SOUL CLOTHED WITH AIR.

SHE was standing, in her chaste nudity, with uplifted arms, twisting the thick and waving masses of her hair, which she was trying to bring into subjection on the top of her head,—a fresh, young beauty, who had not yet attained the fulness and perfection of developed form, but was approaching it, radiant in the loveliness of her seventeenth year.

A child of Venice, her white, soft, rose-tinted skin revealed the circulation of a strong and ardent life-blood beneath its transparency; her eyes shone with a mysterious and haunting light, and the dewy redness of her lightly parted lips made one think of the fruit as much as of the flower. She was marvellously beautiful as she stood thus; and if some hero Paris had received a mission to award the palm to her, I do not know which he would have laid at her feet, that of grace, elegance, or beauty,—for she seemed to blend the living charm of modern attractiveness with the calm perfections of classic beauty.

The happiest, the most unexpected chance had led the painter Falero and me to where she was. One lovely afternoon last spring we were walking on the seashore. We had been through one of the groves of olive-trees, with their sad-looking leaves, which are so frequent between Nice and Monaco, and without being aware of it had entered some private grounds which were unenclosed on the side towards the beach. A picturesque, winding path led up the hill. We had just passed an orange-grove whose golden apples recalled the garden of the Hesperides; the air was fragrant, the sky a deep blue, and we were discoursing upon a parallel between art and science, when my companion suddenly stopped, as if by an irresistible fascination, making me a sign to be silent and to look.

Behind the clumps of cactus and fig-trees, a few feet in front of us, was a sumptuous bathroom, with its western window open, letting us see the young girl standing not far from a marble basin into which a jet of water fell with a gentle murmur, and before a large mirror which reflected her image from head to foot. Probably the noise of the falling water had prevented her hearing our footsteps. We stood mute and motionless behind the cactus, discreetly, or indiscreetly, watching her. She was lovely, and apparently unaware of her own beauty. Her feet were on a tiger-skin; she was in no haste. Finding that her hair was still too damp, she let it fall about her again, turned in our direction, and picked up a rose from the table near the window; then going back to the long mirror, she resumed her hair-dressing, finished it leisurely, put the little rose between two coils, and turning with her back to the sun, stooped, probably to pick up her first piece of clothing. But she suddenly sprang back with a piercing cry, hid her face in her hands, and hastily retreated to a shaded corner.

We have always thought since that some movement of our heads must have betrayed our presence, or that by some trick of the mirror she had seen us. Whatever it was, we thought it prudent to retrace our steps, and went down to the sea again by the same path.

*****

"Ah," said my companion, "I assure you that among all my models I have never seen any more perfect, even for my picture of the 'Double Stars' and of 'Celia.' What do you think about it yourself? Did not that apparition come just in time to prove that I am right? You need waste no eloquence upon the delights of science,—acknowledge that art also has its charms. Do not the stars of Earth compare favorably with the beauties of the sky? Do you not admire the graceful beauty of that form as I do? What exquisite tints, what flesh!"

"I should not have the bad taste not to admire what is truly beautiful," I answered. "I admit that human beauty (and of course female loveliness in particular) truly represents the most perfect thing that Nature has produced on our planet. But do you know what I most admire in that being? It is not its artistic or æsthetic aspect, it is the scientific proof it gives of a simply wonderful fact. In that beautiful body I see a soul clothed with air."

"Oh, you are fond of paradoxes! A soul clothed with air! That is rather idealistic for so real a body! No doubt the charming creature has a soul; but permit an artist to admire her body, her vitality, her solidity, her color...."

"I do not object. But it is just that physical beauty which makes me admire the soul in her, the invisible force that formed her."

"What do you mean by that? We surely have a body! The existence of a soul is less palpable."

"To the senses, yes; to the mind, no. Now, your senses absolutely deceive you about the motion of the Earth, the nature of the sky, the apparent solidity of the body; about beings and about things. Will you follow my reasoning for a moment?

*****

"When I breathe the perfume of a rose, when I admire the beauty of form, the smoothness of coloring, the grace of this flower in its freshly opening bloom, what strikes me most is the work of the hidden, unknown, mysterious force which rules over the plant's life and can direct it in the maintenance of its existence, which chooses the proper molecules of air, water, and earth for its nourishment, and which knows above all how to assimilate those molecules and group them so delicately as to form this graceful stem, these dainty little green leaves, these soft pink petals, these exquisite tints and delicious fragrance. This mysterious force is the animating principle of the plant. Put a lily-seed, an acorn, a grain of wheat, and a peach-stone side by side in the ground; each germ will build up its own organism.

"I knew a maple-tree which was dying on the ruins of an old wall, a few feet from good, rich soil in a ditch, and which in despair threw out a venturesome root, reached the coveted soil, buried itself there, and gained a solid footing, so that by degrees, although a motionless thing, it changed its place, let its original roots die, left the stones, and lived resuscitated upon the organ that had set it free. I have known elms which were going to eat up the soil of a fertile field, whose food had been cut off from them by a wide ditch, and who therefore determined to make their uncut roots pass under the ditch. They succeeded, and returned to their regular food, much to the cultivator's astonishment. I knew an heroic jasmine which went eight times through holes in a board which kept the light away from it, and which a teasing observer would put back into the shade, hoping at last to wear out the flower's energy; but he did not succeed.

"A plant breathes, drinks, eats, selects, refuses, seeks, works, lives, acts according to its instincts. One does 'like a charm,' another pines, a third is nervous and agitated. The sensitive-plant shivers and droops its leaves at the slightest touch. In certain hours of well-being the calla lily is warm, the pink is phosphorescent, the valisneria goes down to the bottom of the lake to ripen the fruit of her loves. In these manifestations of an unknown life the philosopher cannot help recognizing a song from the universal choir in the plant world.

"I go no further for the human soul just now, although it is incomparably superior to the soul of a plant, and although it has created an intellectual world as much above the rest of the terrestrial world as the stars are higher than the Earth. I am not looking at it now from the point of view of its spiritual faculties, but only as force animating the human being.

"Ah! I wonder that that force can group the atoms that we breathe, or that we assimilate by nutrition and form this charming being! Think of that young girl the day she was born, and follow in thought the gradual development of that little body through the years of her awkward age to the first graces of youth and the charms of womanhood. How is human organism nourished, developed, and composed? You know,—by respiration and nutrition.

"The air supplies three quarters of our nourishment by respiration. The oxygen in the air maintains the fire of life, and the body is comparable to a flame, constantly renewed by the principles of combustion. The lack of oxygen extinguishes life as it extinguishes a lamp. By respiration the black venous blood is transformed into red arterial blood and regenerated. The lungs are a fine tissue pierced with from forty to fifty millions of little holes, which are just too small for the blood to filter through, and just large enough for the air to penetrate them. A perpetual interchange of gas takes place between the air and the blood, the first furnishing the second with oxygen, the second eliminating carbonic acid. On the one hand the atmospheric oxygen burns carbon in the lung; on the other the lung exhales carbonic acid, nitrogen, and water in the form of vapor. In the daytime, plants breathe by an opposite process,—they absorb carbonic acid and exhale oxygen; by this difference maintaining one part of the general equilibrium of terrestrial life.

"Of what is the human body composed? An average adult man weighs 70 kilograms. Of this amount there are nearly 52 kilograms of water in the blood and flesh. Analyze the substance of our body, you will find albumen, fibrine, caseine, and gelatine; that is, organic substances composed originally of the four essential gases,—oxygen, nitrogen, hydrogen, and carbonic acid. You will also find substances with no nitrogen, such as gum, sugar, starch, and fat. These matters likewise pass through our organism; their carbon and hydrogen are consumed by the oxygen breathed in during respiration, and then exhaled under the form of carbonic acid and water.

"You are not unaware that water is a combination of two gases, oxygen and hydrogen; the air is a mixture of two gases, oxygen and nitrogen, to which are added in lesser proportions water in the form of vapor, which, however, is but condensed oxygen, etc.

"Thus our body is composed only of transformed gases."

*****

"But," interrupted my companion, "we do not live solely upon the air; at certain hours, indicated by our stomachs, it is very necessary to add some supplies which are not without a value of their own,—such as a pheasant's wing, a filet de sole, a glass of Château Laffitte or champagne, or, as your taste may prefer, asparagus, grapes, peaches...."

"Yes, that all passes through our organism and renews its tissues,—pretty rapidly too; for in a few months (not in seven years, as was formerly thought) our body is entirely renewed. To return to that lovely being who posed before us just now. None of that flesh which we admired existed three or four months ago; those shoulders, that face, those eyes, that mouth, those arms, that hair, and, even to the very nails, all that organism, is but a current of molecules, a ceaselessly renewed flame, a river which we may look at all our lives, but never see the same water again. Now, all that is but assimilated gas, condensed and modified, and more than anything else, it is air. These bones themselves, so solid now, were formed and hardened gradually. Do not forget that our whole body is composed of invisible molecules which do not touch each other, and which are continually renewed.

"Finally, our table is spread with vegetables and fruits; if we are vegetarians we absorb substances almost entirely drawn from the air. This peach is air and water; this pear, this grape, this almond are also made of air and water, a few gaseous elements drawn to them by the sap, by solar heat, by the rain. Asparagus or salad, peas or beans, lettuce or chicory, all these live in the air and on the air; what the earth furnishes, what the sap seeks out, are also gases, and the very same nitrogen, oxygen, hydrogen, carbon, etc.

"If it is a question of beefsteak, chicken, or some other 'meat,' the difference is not very great. Sheep and oxen feed upon grass. If we relish a partridge cooked with cauliflower, a roasted quail, a truffled turkey, or a stewed hare, all these substances, apparently so different, are only transformed vegetable matter, which itself is but a grouping of molecules taken from the gases of which we have just been speaking,—air, water, elements, molecules, and atoms almost imponderable of themselves, and moreover absolutely invisible to the naked eye.

"Thus, whatever may be our kind of nourishment, our body, kept repaired, developed by the absorption of molecules acquired by respiration and alimentation, is really but a current incessantly renewed by means of this assimilation,—directed, governed, and organized by the immaterial force which animates us. To this force we may assuredly give the name of 'soul.' It groups the atoms which suit it, eliminates those which are useless to it, and, starting with an imperceptible speck, an indiscernible germ, ends by building up the Apollo Belvidere or the Venus of the Capitol. Phidias is but a coarse imitator, compared to this hidden and mysterious force. Mythology tells us that Pygmalion became the lover of a statue of his own creation. Not so! Pygmalion, Praxiteles, Michael Angelo, Benvenuto, and Canova created nothing but statues. The force that can construct the living body of man and woman is more sublime.

"But this force is immaterial, invisible, intangible, imponderable, like the attraction which lulls the worlds in the universal melody; and the body, however material it may seem to us, is in itself only a harmonious grouping, formed by the attraction of this interior force. So you see that I confine myself strictly within the limits of positive science in speaking of this young girl by the title of a soul clothed with air,—like you or me, for instance, neither more nor less.

"From the origin of humanity down to within a century or two, it has been believed that sensation was perceived at the very point where it was felt. A pain felt in the finger was considered as having its seat in the finger itself. Children and many people believe so still. Physiology has demonstrated that the impression is transmitted from the finger-tip to the brain by means of the nervous system. If the nerve is cut, the finger may be burned with impunity; the paralysis is complete. We have been able to determine the time taken by the impression in transmitting itself from any part of the body to the brain, and it is known that the rapidity of this transmission is about twenty-eight metres per second. Since then we have referred sensation to the brain. But we have stopped half way.

"The brain is matter, like the finger, and by no means fixed and stable matter. It is essentially changing matter, rapidly variable, and forming no identity. A single lobe, a single cell, a single molecule which does not change, does not and could not exist in the whole mass of encephalic matter. A stoppage of motion, of circulation, or of transformation would be a death-warrant. The brain subsists and feels, only on condition of submitting, like all the rest of the body, to the incessant transformations of organic matter which constitute the vital circuit.

"So it cannot be that our personality, our identity, lies in a certain grouping of cerebral matter,—our individual me, our *ego* which acquires and preserves a personal scientific and moral value, increasing with study; our *ego* which feels itself responsible for its acts performed a month, a year, ten, twenty, fifty years ago, during which time however the molecular grouping has been *changed* frequently.

"Physiologists who affirm that the soul does not exist, are like their ancestors who affirmed that they felt pain in their finger or their foot. They are a little less far from the truth, but they stop on the way when they stop at the brain, and make the human being consist of cerebral impressions. This hypothesis is all the less excusable because these same physiologists know perfectly well that personal sensation is always accompanied by a modification of substance. In other words, the *ego* of the individual only continues when the identity of its matter ceases to continue.

"Our principle of sensibility, then, cannot be a material object; it is put in communication with the universe by cerebral impressions, by the chemical forces disengaged in the encephalon in consequence of material combinations. But it is *different.*

"And our organic constitution is perpetually transformed under the direction of a psychic principle.

"Some molecule now incorporated in our organism escapes from it by expiration, perspiration, etc., to belong to the atmosphere for a longer or shorter time, then to be incorporated into another organism,—plant, animal, or man. The molecules which actually constitute your body were not all made part of your person yesterday, and none of them were there three months ago. Where were they? Either in the air or in another body. All the molecules now forming your organic tissues, your lungs, your eyes, your brain, your legs, etc., have already served to form other organic tissues. We are all resuscitated dead men, made from the dust of our ancestors. If all the people who have lived up to this time arose from the dead, there would be five of them to every square foot upon the surface of all the continents,—obliged to climb on one another's shoulders in order to stand; but they could not all be completely resuscitated, for many of the molecules have served successively for several bodies.

"Our own organisms likewise, resolved into their ultimate particles, will help to form the bodies of our descendants.

"Each molecule of air then goes on eternally from life to life, and escapes thence from death to death, by turns wind, wave, earth, animal, or flower. It is incorporated successively into the substance of numberless organisms. The air, the inexhaustible source whence everything that lives takes its breath, is yet an immense reservoir into which everything that dies pours its last sigh; by its absorption, vegetable and animal, different organisms come to life and afterwards perish. Life and death are both in the air we breathe, and perpetually succeed each other by the exchange of gaseous molecules; the molecule of oxygen which this old oak exhales will fly away to the lungs of a child in its cradle. The last sighs of a man will weave the brilliant corolla of a flower, or expand like a smile over the verdant meadow. And thus by an infinite series of partial deaths, the atmosphere incessantly nourishes the universal life spread over the surface of the world.

"And if nevertheless some objection should still remain unanswered, I would go further, and add that our clothes as well as our bodies are composed of substances which at first were all gaseous. Take this thread, draw it out: what a resistance! How many webs of cambric, silk, linen, cotton, and wool industry have been formed by the help of these warps and woofs! And yet, what is a thread of linen, flax, or cotton? Globules of air in juxtaposition which are held together only by their molecular force. What is a thread of silk or wool? Another set of molecules in juxtaposition. Admit, then, that our clothes as well are air, gas, substances drawn in the beginning from the atmosphere,—oxygen, nitrogen, carbon, vapor of water, etc."

*****

"I am glad to see," said the painter, "that art is not so far from science as is supposed in certain circles. If your theory is purely scientific to you, to me it is art, and of the best. Besides, do all these distinctions exist in Nature? In Nature there is neither art nor painting nor sculpture, music nor decoration, philosophy nor chemistry, nor astronomy nor meteorology. Look at the sky, the sea, those foot-hills of the Alps, those rosy evening clouds, those luminous perspectives towards the Italian coast,—all that is one. There is unity in everything. And since molecular philosophy demonstrates that there is no longer any body, that even the atoms in a bar of steel or platinum do not touch each other, no one will be the loser, provided our souls are left us."

"Yes, it is a fact against which no prejudice can prevail,—living beings are souls clothed with air. I pity the worlds deprived of their atmosphere."

We had returned to the seashore after a long ramble not far from our point of departure, and were passing the battlemented wall of a villa on our way from Beaulieu to Cape Ferrat, when two very fashionably dressed ladies passed us. They were the Duchess of V—— and her daughter, whom we had met the previous Thursday at a ball at the Préfecture. We bowed to them, and disappeared under the olive-trees. The young girl, inquisitive daughter of Eve, turned to look after us, and it seemed to me that a sudden blush crimsoned her cheeks; it was doubtless the reflection of the setting sun's rays.

"Perhaps you think," said the artist, also looking back, "that you have diminished my admiration for beauty? No, I appreciate it still more. In it I bow to harmony; and—shall I confess it?—the human body thus considered as the manifestation to the senses of a directing soul seems to me to acquire thence more nobility, more beauty, and more light."

V.
AD VERITATEM PER SCIENTIAM.

I WAS studying in my library the conditions of life upon the surface of worlds governed and illuminated by suns of different sizes, when glancing at the chimney-piece I was struck with the expression—I had almost said the animation—of my dear Urania's face. It was the gracious, living expression which once—ah! how quickly the earth goes round, and how short a quarter of a century is!—which once—and it seems to me like yesterday—which once—in those youthful days so quickly flown—had attracted my thoughts and inflamed my heart. I could not keep from looking at her again, and resting my eyes on her. Truly, she was still just as beautiful, and my feelings had not changed. She drew me to her as the light draws an insect. I rose from my table to approach her, and see again the singular effect of the daylight on her changing face, and I surprised myself by standing before her, forgetting my work.

Her look seemed to be lost in the distance, yet she was looking. At what? I had the firm conviction that she was really looking at something; and following the direction of that fixed, motionless, solemn, although not severe gaze, my eyes went straight to Spero's portrait, hanging there between two book-cases. Really, Urania was looking fixedly at him.

Suddenly the picture broke away from the wall and fell, breaking the frame. I rushed to it. The portrait was lying on the carpet, and Spero's gentle face was turned towards me. Picking it up, I found a large paper, grown yellow, which filled up the whole back, and was written over on both sides in Spero's handwriting. Why had I never noticed this paper? It is true that it might have lain under the setting of the frame, hidden beneath the protecting cardboard mat. When I brought this water-color back from Christiania I did not think of examining its arrangement. But who could have had the singular idea of putting this sheet in such a place? I recognized my friend's handwriting, and glanced over the two pages in utter bewilderment. According to all appearances they must have been written on the last day of the young student's life,—the day of his ascension to the aurora borealis. Probably Icléa's father wished to preserve these last thoughts carefully, so framed them with Spero's portrait, and forgot to mention it when he afterwards gave me the portrait as a memento, on my return from the pilgrimage to my two friends' graves. However that might be, placing the water-color gently on the table, I experienced the deepest emotion as I recognized every detail of that dear face. They were his very eyes, so sweet, so deep, and always unfathomable; the wide brow apparently so calm, the delicate mouth with its reserved sensitiveness, the fresh coloring of the face, neck, and hands. His eyes looked at me, whichever way I turned the portrait; they looked at Urania at the same time; they looked everywhere at once. Strange idea of the artist! I could not resist the thought of Urania's eyes, which had seemed to me to be looking at the portrait with embarrassing intentness. Her celestial countenance no longer wore the same expression at all, but appeared to me rather to be melancholy, almost sad. Then I turned again to the mysterious sheet of paper. It was written in a clear, precise hand, with no erasures. I offer it to the readers of this book just as I found it, without the slightest change; for it appears to be the very natural conclusion of the preceding episodes.

Here it is, *verbatim*:—

This is the scientific testament of a mind which on the Earth did all in its power to remain independent of the weight of matter, and which hopes to be freed from it.

I should like to leave the results of my researches in the form of aphorisms. It seems to me that the Truth can be reached only through the study of Nature, that is to say, by science. Here are the inductions which appear to me to be founded on this method of observation.

I.

The visible, tangible, ponderable, and constantly moving universe is composed of invisible, intangible, imponderable, and inert atoms.

II.

These atoms are governed by force, to constitute bodies and to organize beings.

III.

Force is essential entity.

IV.

Visibility, tangibility, solidity, and weight are relative properties, and not absolute realities.

V.

The infinitely small.

The experiments made in beating gold-leaf show that ten thousand leaves are contained in the thickness of a millimetre. A millimetre has been divided on a glass plate into a thousand equal parts; and infusoria exist, which are so small that their entire bodies, placed between two of these divisions, do not touch either of them. The members and organs of these beings are composed of cellules, these of molecules, and these of atoms. Twenty cubic centimetres of oil spread over a lake will cover four thousand square metres, so that the layer of oil thus expanded measures only one two hundred thousandth of a millimetre in thickness. Spectral analysis of light discloses the presence of a millionth of a milligramme of sodium in a flame. The sense of smell perceives 1/604000000 a milligramme of mercaptan in the air breathed. The dimensions of atoms must be less than a millionth of a millimetre in diameter. [Waves of light are comprised between 4 and 8 ten millionths of a millimetre, from violet to red; 2300 are required to fill a millimetre. In the duration of a second the ether through which light is transmitted makes 700,000,000,000,000 oscillations, each of which is mathematically defined.]

VI.

The intangible, invisible atom, scarcely conceivable to our mind accustomed to superficial judgments, constitutes the only true matter; and what we call matter is but an effect produced on our senses by the motion of atoms,— that is to say, an incessant possibility of sensations.

The result is, that matter, like the manifestations of energy, is only a mode of motion. If motion should stop; if force should be annihilated; if the temperature of bodies should be reduced to absolute zero,—matter, as we know it, would cease to exist.

VII.

The visible universe is composed of invisible bodies. What we see is made up of things which are not seen. There is but one kind of primitive atom. The constituent molecules of different bodies—iron, gold, oxygen, hydrogen, etc.—differ only in the number, grouping, and motion of the atoms which compose them.

VIII.

What we call "matter," vanishes when scientific analysis thinks to grasp it. But we find as the support of the universe and the origin of all form, Force,—the dynamic element. By my will I can unsettle the Moon in her course.

The movements of each atom on our Earth are the mathematical resultant of the undulations of the luminiferous ether which come to it in time from the abysses of infinite space.

IX.

The human being has for essential principle the soul. The body is visible and transitory.

X.

Atoms are indestructible.

The energy which moves atoms and governs the universe is indestructible.

The human soul is indestructible.

XI.

The individuality of the soul is recent in the Earth's history. Our planet was nebula, then sun, after that, chaos. No terrestrial human being was then in existence. Life began with the most rudimentary organisms; it has progressed century by century to attain its present state, which is not the last. What we call the faculties of the soul,—intelligence, reason, conscience,—are modern. The mind has gradually freed itself from matter; as—if the comparison were not awkward—gas frees itself from coal, perfume from the flower, flame from fire.

XII.

Psychic force has been beginning to assert itself in the higher spheres of terrestrial humanity for the past thirty or forty centuries; its action is but in its dawn. Souls conscious of their individuality, or still unconscious of it, are by their very nature beyond the conditions of space and time. After the death of the body, as during life, they occupy no place; perhaps some of them go to dwell in other worlds. Those only who are freed from material bonds can be conscious of their extra-corporeal existence and immortality.

XIII.

The Earth is but a province of the eternal fatherland; it forms a part of heaven. *Heaven is infinite*; all worlds are a part of heaven.

XIV.

The planetary and sidereal systems which constitute the universe are at different degrees of organization and advancement. The extent of their diversity is infinite; beings are everywhere appropriate to their worlds.

XV.

All worlds are not lived upon. The present era is of no more importance than are those which preceded or those which will follow it. Some worlds have been inhabited in the past, others will be in the future. Some day nothing will remain of the Earth; even its ruins will have perished.

XVI.

Terrestrial life is not the type of other lives. An unlimited diversity reigns in the universe. There are dwelling-places where the weight is intense, where light is unknown, where touch, smell, and hearing are the only senses, where, the optic nerve not being formed, all the beings are blind. There are others where the beings are so light and so slight that they would be invisible to earthly eyes, where senses of an exquisite delicacy reveal to privileged beings sensations forbidden to terrestrial humanity.

XVII.

The space existing between the worlds distributed over the immense universe does not separate them from each other. They are all in perpetual communication, from the attraction which makes itself felt through all distance, and establishes an indissoluble link between all worlds.

XVIII.

The universe forms a single unity.

XIX.

The system of the physical world is the material basis, the habitat of the moral or spiritual world. Hence astronomy must be the basis of all philosophical and religious belief. Every thinking being bears within himself the consciousness, but the uncertainty, of immortality. This is because we are the microscopic wheels of an unknown mechanism.

XX.

Man makes his own destiny. He rises or falls in accordance with his works. Beings attached to material riches, misers, hypocrites, liars, ambitious people, live like the perverse, in the lower zones.

But a primordial and absolute law governs creation,—the law of Progress. Everything rises in the infinite. Sins are falls.

XXI.

In the ascension of souls, moral qualities have no less value than intellectual qualities. Goodness, devotion, self-abnegation, sacrifice, purify the soul, and raise it, like study and science.

XXII.

Universal creation is an immense harmony, of which the Earth is but an insignificant, rather uninteresting, and unfinished fragment.

XXIII.

Nature is a perpetual future. *Progress is law.* Progression is eternal.

XXIV.

The eternity of a soul would not be long enough to visit the infinite and learn all there is to know.

XXV.

The soul's destiny is to free itself more and more from the material world, and to belong to the lofty Uranian life, whence it can look down upon matter and suffer no more. It then enters upon the spiritual life, eternally pure. The supreme aim of all beings is the perpetual approach to absolute perfection and divine happiness.

Such was Spero's scientific and philosophical testament. Does it not seem to have been dictated by Urania herself?

The Nine Muses of ancient mythology were sisters. Modern scientific conceptions in their turn tend to unity. Astronomy, or the knowledge of the world, and psychology, or knowledge of being, unite to-day to establish the only basis on which definite philosophy can be built.

*****

P. S.—The preceding incidents, with the researches and reflections which accompany them, are brought together here in a sort of essay, whose aim is to shed a gleam of light on the solution of the greatest problem that can engage the human mind. With this object the present work is offered to the attention of those who sometimes "in the midst of Life's journey," of which Dante speaks, linger to ask themselves where and what they are,—to seek, to think, and to dream.

Footnotes

[1] Strange coincidences sometimes occur; and upon the day that George Spero made the ascent which was to be so fatal to him I knew that he had started, from the extraordinary restlessness of the magnetic needle, which announced at Paris, where I had remained, the intense aurora borealis for which he had been waiting so anxiously to make his aerial journey. It is well known that the aurora borealis causes magnetic disturbances which are felt at long distances from their manifestation. But what surprised me most, and what I never have been able to explain, is, that at the very time of the accident I experienced an undefined uneasiness; then a kind of presentiment that some accident had happened to him. The despatch announcing his death found me almost prepared for it.

[2] Phantasms of the Living. By E. Gurney and Frederick Myers, of the University of Cambridge, and Frank Podmore. London, 1886. (The president of the Society for Psychical Research is Professor Balfour Stewart, F. R. S.)

Milton Keynes UK
Ingram Content Group UK Ltd.
UKHW030624061024
449204UK00004B/346